The Social Ski.

2 In 1

How To Make It Past A 30 Second Conversation And Leave A Great First Impression

By

Chad Collins

Table of Contents

The Social-Skills Cure

Conversation Hacks

The Social Skills Cure

How To Engage In Conversation With
People Who Don't Know You Well Even If
You're Naturally Shy

By

Chad Collins

Introduction

Millions of people throughout the nation are shy. They suffer from immense social anxiety and low self-esteem that prevents them from going out, making friends, getting their dream job and just having the quality lifestyle that they desire.

Social anxiety does not come with any symptoms you can see from a mile away. Millions of people suffer and for most of them, you would never be able to tell there is any problem but deep inside they are fighting an internal battle that rages on every day.

If you suffer from social anxiety, it may seem like you are drowning, like there is no way that you can get out. Fortunately, there is a solution. There are numerous studies that highlight the causes and the solutions for social anxiety and there are strategies you can implement every day.

As a researcher who has not only spent years looking into different types of anxiety, but has also experienced and overcome social anxiety, I am here to help you find answers.

Social anxiety does not have to take over your life. Have you ever looked at people who are so outgoing, always smiling and saying hello to people they have never met, and wondered what makes them able to do this? What makes them so confident? I can help you discover the key to unlocking your inner self-confidence and overcome the shyness, low self-esteem and social anxiety that prevent you from socializing once and for all.

The strategies and skills explained in this book have been heavily researched by top scientists, psychologists and universities who have spent years trying to discover the causes and effects of social anxiety and further understand these conditions for the good of society.

While I cannot promise you that every single thing discussed in this book will work for you, I can promise that this book will give you a place to start. Here you will find the basics of where these conditions start and some practical skills you can implement in your daily life to put your social anxiety to an end.

The longer you wait, the more life is passing you by. There are places to go, people to see and things to do. Without the social skills to face life head-on, time is going to go on without you.

So go ahead and read on and as you do make a commitment that this will be the moment that changes your life for the better.

Tackling The Mental Barriers To Socializing

Seeing The Effects Of Shyness, Anxiety, Poor Self-Confidence And Discouragement

Factors such as shyness, anxiety, poor self-confidence and discouragement can be debilitating to your quality of life leading to reduced social life and lack of opportunity due to not taking chances.

A common perception about shyness is that it is just a phase, something that is learned sometime during childhood or adolescence and people outgrow it with time. While this is possible, it is more than likely not the case.[3]

In reality, 40 to 60 percent of adults consider themselves shy, according to Psych Central. Although shyness can begin during childhood, 10 to 15 percent of people even develop shyness during infancy, for most people shyness is something that is learned later in life. [3]

Shyness can affect anyone, but the majority of shy people are adolescents, particularly girls, due to self-consciousness because of bodily changes and a new focus on self and privacy.

Another common perception of shy people is that they all outwardly exhibit characteristics of shy people. However, most shy people can be considered extroverted, at least on the outside. They feel comfortable in a social situation as long as they are in a situation where they are in control of the situation. [3]

Despite this, on the inside, they are self-conscious, have negative feelings about their appearance and their behaviors, are preoccupied with what others think of them and exhibit physical symptoms such as increased heart rate and pulse and the feeling of butterflies in their stomach when placed in social situations.

According to Psychology Today, only about 15 to 20 percent of people actually fit the typical description of a shy person who expresses their shyness through their behaviors such as being visibly nervous when talking to people and using excuses to get out of social situations. [4]

Meanwhile, 80 to 85 percent of people are privately shy, Psychology Today says. They don't show the behavioral characteristics of a shy person. Instead, these traits are shown within them and they can wreak personal havoc. While they seem confident in conversation, on the inside have had self-deprecating inner dialogue and question whether the person they are talking to really likes them. [4]

It is important to note, however, that shyness and introvertedness are not the same things. Introverts actually possess the necessary conversational skills as well as self-esteem to interact with others on a daily basis although they actually prefer to be alone. Shy people want to be with other people but they lack the necessary confidence and social skills to do so.

There are a number of negative consequences that come with shyness that can result in negative effects on your physical health, effects on your career choice and the amount of money you make and your overall quality of life.

Some of the ways shyness can be affecting your life are:[4]

- **Loneliness**

Due to the isolation that shy people experience, it is likely that they have no circle of close friends. They do not have anyone to talk to in times of need or go out with which further isolates them from the rest of the world. Because of their loneliness, shy people are at risk for physical and mental decline.

- **Vulnerability**

Also because they do not have any close friends or role models to correct their behavior and keep them on a good path, shy people are more vulnerable to dangerous and risky behaviors.

- **Drug and alcohol abuse**

  Because they are at risk of more dangerous behaviors, shy people are more likely to succumb to peer pressure in an attempt to feel like they belong which can lead to using drugs and alcohol. Shy people can also be led to use in an attempt to get rid of feelings of loneliness and find a sense of self-acceptance.

- **Wasting time**

  Shy people tend to spend a lot of time over-analyzing social situations. They are consumed with thoughts of the future and its consequences that they end up not living in the moment.

Low self-confidence, or self-esteem, is a contributing factor to shyness. Self-esteem is how people feel about themselves and when people have low self-esteem they rely on how they do in the present to define how they feel about themselves. They need positive external experiences, such as compliments from people around them, to feel good about themselves although, to people with low self-esteem, good feelings about themselves are temporary. [17]

Self-esteem evolves throughout people's lives through experiences and their environment. Childhood experiences such as being listened to, being spoken to respectfully, being given the appropriate level of attention and affection and being recognized and accepted for accomplishments and mistakes all contribute to healthy self-esteem later in life. If one experiences things like harsh criticism, abuse, being ignored, ridiculed or teased or being given high expectations, they are more likely to have low self-esteem later in life. [17]

Low self-confidence usually displays itself in three ways: [17]

- **Putting On A Façade**

People who display their low self-confidence in this way act like they are happy and successful but in reality, they are terrified of failure. Not only this, but they live in constant fear of their cover being blown and people finding out how insecure they really are. They need continuous successes in their life to feel positive self-esteem and usually exhibit traits of perfectionism, procrastination, competition and burn out.

- **Rebelliousness**

  People who display their low self-confidence in this way act like the opinions of others have no effect on them. However, they are in a state of constant anger over not being good enough. They feel the need to prove that people's criticisms don't really hurt them. They are constantly blaming others, breaking rules and opposing authority because of this.

- **Playing The Victim**

  These people act like they are helpless because of their low self-confidence. They want someone to rescue them instead of having to take responsibility for their actions and use pity as a shield for not taking responsibility. Oftentimes they look to others for guidance. They are usually unassertive, underachievers and rely on others.

Some of the other consequences of low self-confidence include problems forming meaningful friendships and romantic relationships, failures in academics or job performance, increased vulnerability to drug and alcohol abuse, negative self-image and actively destructive behavior.

One of the consequences of low self-confidence is anxiety. As the most common mental illness in the U.S., 40 million adults suffer from some form of an anxiety disorder, according to the Anxiety and Depression Association of America. Anxiety disorders are highly treatable, however; only about 37 percent of the population actually gets treated for their anxiety which develops from a variety of factors such as genetics, brain chemistry, personality and certain life events. [1]

As our understanding of anxiety continues to grow through current research and admitting to having anxiety and getting treatment becomes more accepted in our society, anxiety has an increasing influence in contemporary life as it is increasingly recognized. [1]

Prominent people are becoming public about their struggles with anxiety in an attempt to help others. Support groups and education serve to make people more aware of what anxiety is and how to treat it making it slowly become less stigmatized. It is also more reflected in our literature, arts, science and other aspects of our culture more than ever. [21]

Anxiety research has been around for centuries, but the modern understanding of anxiety emerged around the 20th century where scientists began to look at it as an explicit, pervasive problem. This was because of a variety of social and cultural factors, such as the wars and social conflicts of the time period, that undermined one's sense of personal security and people generally developed problems with establishing their own psychological identity. All of these factors contributed to a heightened vulnerability to anxiety by society as a whole. [21]

From there, anxiety began to be recognized not only as a single disorder but a contributing factor to other physical problems such as lack of sleep, psychological symptoms and lack of creative self-expression.

There are many different anxiety disorders such as generalized anxiety disorder, panic disorder and specific phobias, but social anxiety disorder can develop out of shyness and can be detrimental to a person who is already shy. Social anxiety disorder is the second most diagnosed anxiety disorder after specific phobias. [21]

Social anxiety disorder is when a person gets intense anxiety or fear of being judged, negatively evaluated or rejected in social or performance situations and it leads them to try to avoid social situations at all costs and feel anxiety or stress when they have no choice but to be involved in the social situation which causes their fear With social anxiety disorder, people worry about being visibly anxious about being viewed as stupid, awkward or boring in social situations. [1]

Throughout the United States, about 15 million adults suffer from a social anxiety disorder, that's about 6.8 percent of the population, and signs of social anxiety disorder usually begin around the age of 13, especially in youths who are extremely shy. [1]

Some of the physical symptoms of a social anxiety disorder include rapid heart rate, nausea, sweating and even anxiety attacks. Additionally, people with the disorder recognize that their fears are unwarranted; however, they cannot control these feelings and feel powerless to stop them.

There are endless situations where people may experience signs of social anxiety disorder. A few of them are: [1]

- Meeting new people
- Dating
- Job Interviews
- Answering questions in class
- Talking to Cashiers
- Interacting with co-workers

- Speaking to acquaintances you don't know well
- Giving a presentation or speeches
- Attending meetings
- Going to parties

Because symptoms of social anxiety disorder are so strong, people may worry about planned situations or anticipated situations they may find themselves in for weeks prior only prolonging their anxiety longer than needed. The disorder can run in families, but some may also be predisposed to social anxiety or may misread other people's behaviors leading them to think that others think little of them. Unfortunately, fewer than five percent of people who suffer from social anxiety disorder actually end up getting help for the disorder or they usually get help after ten years or more of suffering.

These intense fears of social situations can have a devastating effect on a person's life such as:
- Declining job opportunities that require interaction with people

— Depending on the people I will gladly hang-out w/ them.

- Avoiding hanging out with friends
- Disrupting daily routines or occupational performance
- Difficulty developing friendships and relationships
- Risk for major depressive disorder and alcohol abuse

Shifting Your Mindset About Your Social Discomfort

Shyness, self-confidence issues, anxiety and discouragement can have a debilitating effect on your everyday life from your relationships and friendships, ability to hold a steady job that you enjoy to simply how you view yourself. However, there is hope. Different types of copsing skills and a certain level of risk-taking can begin to bring you out of your shell.

Part of how you can begin to change your mindset surrounding social withdrawal in the present time might come from coping mechanisms. These are the tendency to respond to stressful situations in a predictable manner. They involve a balance of cognitive and behavioral components. [13]

There are three different categories of coping skills that will help you begin to step out of your comfort zone and change your mindset when it comes to shyness, with some being more helpful to shyness than others: [13]

- **Task-Oriented Skills**

These are skills that have to do with problems solving.

- **Avoidance-Oriented Skills**

These skills involve avoiding the stressor. If someone asks you to hang out with friends, you might decline the invitation saying you have something else to do. Or if you find yourself about to walk into a room where there are a lot of people, you may avoid the situation by going to a quieter room and engaging in an activity that you can do on your own.

- **Emotion-Oriented Skills**

These involve focusing on your internal emotional state. However, if not done correctly, these skills can inhibit progress in moving away from successfully coping with shyness because your internal emotional state can include negative thoughts and feelings and if you focus on these more than positive thoughts it will be counter-productive.

To diminish your shyness, you want to find strategies that will enable you to build social competence. Building social competence strengthens your social skills by associating with positive factors in your environment. For example, if a child who is vulnerable to shyness has secure and loving caregivers, this can actually strengthen their confidence and build their social competence.

However, as an adult, you sometimes have to go out and find these environmental factors yourself. For a person who suffers from social anxiety, shyness and low self-confidence, this can be very difficult and, for some, it can be downright terrifying. But taking the initiative to put yourself in social situations in small doses can be an extremely beneficial first steps to building social competence and eventually ending social withdrawal.

Some of the ways you can do this are: [13]

- **Finding extracurricular activities**

  This is a great opportunity to find a way to socialize with others. Finding extracurricular activities could mean participating in a team sport or taking a class where others are guaranteed to be there such as a group exercise class or a cooking class. Putting yourself in these situations where more than likely you will have to talk to people on some level will with time enhance your communication skills and reduce the awkwardness you feel when it comes to talking to others.

- **Building peer bonds**

  The more you leave the house and participate in a consistent activity, the more likely you will be to interact with the same people on a regular basis and will be more likely to develop friendships with them because of the common interests you share.

- **Introducing yourself to people**

  Is there a neighbor that you see walking their dog by your house often? Go out one day and say hello. Maybe there is someone you sit next to in class who you have never spoken to before. Initiate conversation and tell them your name. Or maybe you can introduce yourself to a coworker that you sit near. Introducing yourself to people can be a good jumping off point to starting conversations and making friends.

- **Join groups on the internet**

  Although it is not face-to-face interaction, joining a group where you can have regular conversations with people can be good practice for interacting with people in person. After getting to know people, there might even be an opportunity to meet up as a group in person or in a public place and the good thing is you would already know them well and get to skip over the introduction phase.

All of these things come with a certain level of risk-taking. As a shy person, when you hear the word risk you might want to run away as fast as you can, and while the idea can be intimidating it can also be the critical step to moving past social withdrawal.

When people experience social anxiety, they often overthink things. They obsess over what they are going to say in a situation, how they will stand, how long the interaction will take and more. The thing about risk-taking, though, is that it is not based on rational calculations alone. It requires optimism and what can be described as an animal spirit, just going for it without any thought. When taking a risk, it is necessary to try to leave the worries about what is going to happen at the door and go for it. [12]

Risk taking also involves believing in yourself. This is extremely important for any difficult situation that you find yourself in. One of the first steps towards believing in yourself and your ability to take risks involves changes in your perceived self-efficacy, or your perceived ability to make good decisions.

If you believe in yourself in ineffectual, this leads you to believe that you only have the ability to affect limited changes in your environment where opportunities can be available to you. Hand-in-hand with low self-confidence, this leads you to dwell on your own personal deficiencies instead of characteristics that make you unique and able to make changes. You will also be more likely to envision failure scenarios instead of successes which serve to debilitate your ability to take risks.

Self-efficacy has a few other effects on your ability to step out of your comfort zone. It influences your aspirations and your commitment to your goals. It also has an impact on your persistence to complete tasks and your attitude while at work. What is good about self-efficacy though is that actually very teachable. With a little bit a practice and persistence over time, it is very possible to build self-efficacy over time. [12]

With risk-taking also comes your perception of opportunity and your perception of threat. Decision makers usually differ on their interpretation of cues for making the decision causing them to differ on their level of risk taking. Some people, typically those who are considered shy or socially withdrawn, see uncontrollable situations as a threat while those who are more outgoing and more likely to take risks see uncertainty as an opportunity.

However, what makes a situation controllable or uncontrollable is in the eye of the beholder and usually has to do with a person's level of self-efficacy. Higher self-efficacy leads to more risk-taking, more letting go of comfort and more letting go of social withdrawal. Those with a higher self-efficacy do not dwell on the uncontrollable threats and instead frame risky choices as opportunities for growth.

Another thing that factors into risk-taking is decision making. It involves choosing between different alternatives that vary in their perceived return and the probability of achieving the goal of the alternative. [12]

Like risk-taking, a higher self-efficacy leads to a higher perception of the opportunities presented to you and decrease the perception of threat. Because of this, you are more likely to increase risk-taking and opportunities to step away from social withdrawal.

Studies on the origins of social withdrawal are fairly new; most of them did not start to appear until the 1980s. But now that social withdrawal is beginning to be more studied and understood, studies have since founds that there is a strong association between social competence and social acceptance and factors associated with social competence may serve to reduce the fear of peer rejection that often goes hand in hand with shyness. [6]

Recent studies have also found social withdrawal typically begins at a young age developing from a number of environmental factors. These experiences that you have throughout your developmental years promote social competence and increase social confidence in children who are already born with a disposition towards shyness. [6]

If you suffer from any type of social withdrawal or shyness, you might be able to point to experiences throughout your childhood and adolescence that may have had some impact on your level of shyness.

Some studies have shown that the likelihood that a person will be shy begins at conception and after they are born they are predisposed to shyness because of genetics or other environmental factors.

Parents can have some influence on how shy their children end up being. This can have to do with their parenting styles, such as being over-controlling or being over-involved in their children's personal lives, dictating their feelings and actions. Signs of shyness can begin as early as infancy which can also be influenced by parents or caretakers. [6]

If parents are shy, these behaviors can be picked up by their children. Also if the parent is shy, they may not want to interact with others very much causing their children to have limited interaction with other people and end up picking up isolating behaviors. The child can also develop hesitancy and poor social skills from these factors.

In early childhood, children are entering a new level of independence where they are developing social skills as they learn to interact with others and become more confident within themselves. However, if a child is shy, these developmental milestones can be that much harder to accomplish.

Already predisposed to isolationist and hesitant behaviors, shy children are more likely to form poor relationships with their peers and in turn putting them at risk for developing social anxiety, especially at a younger age. If children are able to form more successful relationships with their peers, they are more likely to reduce their level of shyness because they can find support from others as they explore new environments and develop social skills through interaction with people their age.[6]

At this age, children are also learning to identify and discuss their emotions on a more comprehensive level. Emotionality has an effect on the social outcomes that a child will experience. If a child had a positive emotionality, being optimistic and open to new situations, they increase their tendency to positively engage with others. But if they are predisposed to negative emotionality, withdrawn behavior and pessimism towards encountering new people and situations, they are more likely to develop mood disorders such as depression as well as unpredictable shyness.

Positive friendships can serve as a buffer against shyness and depressive tendencies. Developing close friendships from an early age will ensure more positive experiences. However, the lack of positive friendships and low acceptance from peers leads to the loneliness that can become more debilitating later in life. [6]

Finally, in late childhood emotions play a significant role in creating positive relationships and if shy children already struggle with social interaction, this inhibits development. It leads them to develop a poor sense of self where they feel like they do not belong or fit in with their peers and feel uncomfortable in the presence of others. [6]

Shyness is more than anything a manifestation of social withdrawal distinguished by its conflict between approach and avoidance. Shy people have a desire to interact with others but are hesitant for fear of negative outcomes such as fear that others will think they are boring or awkward. Putting into practice a few strategies that can help you step out of your comfort zone is a good way to start.

Handling Counterproductive Thinking About Socializing

Taking risks is essential to progressing in life but it involves changing the way you think. Beginning to overcome social anxiety involves working through your thoughts and mindset before you can begin to put any actions into play.

For someone with social anxiety, the idea of socializing can be intimidating but socializing is actually an important aspect of everyday life for a number of reasons. Socializing involves being a part of or with other people, whether it is one person or a group of people, all the while enjoying their company, confiding in them or letting them confide in you and working together toward shared goals. [9]

Some examples of situations where you might find yourself socializing involve going to church, joining a club or a group, chatting online, calling a friend on the phone or hanging out with friends; pretty much any situation where you find yourself around people, engaging with them and utilizing social skills.

These situations show that social skills are very important because they overall make it easier to socialize and enjoy the benefits of it and the benefits of it are plentiful.

For one thing, socializing banishes loneliness by promoting a sense of safety, belonging and enjoyment that helps people feel secure in themselves. More than that, socializing:[9]

- Helps you feel like you are part of something larger than yourself
- Helps you to feel supported when you need it, especially in tough times.
- Having people to spend time with and share things with: This is especially important because it helps to ward off loneliness in addition to providing entertainment as well as a distraction from pain.
- It makes you feel wanted, included and cared for.
- You have someone to confide in secrets, ideas and feelings.
- Builds confidence
- Strengthens your sense of meaning and purpose in life.
- Raises your spirits

- It protects you against the effects of stress and loss.

  Negative thoughts are a big aspect of shyness and social anxiety. Ideas of negative thing that people they interact with think about them and negative thoughts of the self are detrimental to not only self-confidence but any courage one could have about putting themselves out there to socialize.

  If this sounds like you, there are several actions you can put into place to stop that counteractive thinking dead in its tracks and retain the will power to socialize. [2]

- **Notice and stop thoughts**

  The best way to do this is to stop telling yourself negative things about yourself and thinking that others think little of you. And of course that's hard because it becomes so ingrained in the mind without even realizing it but before you know it you're putting yourself down constantly which has an impact on the mind. But your inner dialogue does not always have to be negative and not useful to a positive mindset. It is what you make of it and you can make it rational and hopeful. A soon as you find a negative thought crossing your mind, react to it with something positive.

- **Ask about thoughts**

When you do experience counterproductive thoughts, ask themselves whether this is actually helpful or unhelpful. If you are telling yourself that you will never be able to talk to the person that you have a crush on because you are incapable because of social anxiety and they will never like you, ask yourself if the evidence really supports these thoughts. Surely you have a number of positive qualities that you could list and there is no evidence that this person would reject you. You can also ask yourself what you can do to improve yourself. Maybe if you smile or ask them about themselves you can gain their interest even more. What can you do, or what are you already doing, that suggests evidence contrary to the negative thoughts you're having?

- **Journaling**

This could be really useful to give you a visual way to examine and engage with the negative thoughts that make you anxious. It will help to see what unhelpful thoughts you are having and allow you to replace them with helpful ones. Write down the counterproductive thoughts you have either throughout the day or at the end of the day. Next to it, write down a helpful message to correct it. One of those negative thoughts might be "I'll never get my dream job because I worry about everything all the time." The correcting helpful thought that you can write next to it can be something like "I have worked hard and am qualified for this position. I can practice letting go of my worries."

One of the main things to keep in mind when it comes to socialization is that it is about the quality of the relationships that you build, not the quantity, that define the benefits of socializing. You can have an endless amount of people around you that you socialize with, but that does not mean that they are necessarily good quality relationships. [2]

It is important to find quality people to spend time with, and this is especially important for shy people who are already vulnerable and in their search for someone to spend time with who will want to have them around, they might ignore the fact that this person or people might not be the best type of person for them to be around. Shy people might end up falling into contact with people who don't have the best intentions for them, might cause the shy person to fall into behaviors that they shouldn't be a part of just because of their desire to fit in and are all around just toxic people.

As you go on your journey to improve your socialization, be on the lookout for deep, caring relationships with people who want to be friends with you because of you who are. Find people who share common interests with you, common life goals and a similar outlook on life. [2]

It also requires you to put in some effort on your part. Show genuine interest in people that you socialize with. Ask questions about them and make a concerted effort to get to know them just as you would hope they do for you. All the while, make an effort to get out of the old headspace that social anxiety and shyness put you in with thoughts that people don't want to be around you or they don't like you for whatever reason. Tell yourself throughout the social interaction that you are interesting, you are good enough and people want to be around you.

Certainly, it is possible to fall into contact with someone who is not compatible with you, but do not let that discourage you from being social and instead of reverting back to old behaviors. Keep putting yourself out there and know that you will succeed.

Strategies For Taking The Edge Off Anxiety

Knowing the benefits that socializing can have on your life and a few ways to overcome it mentally is all well and good, but knowing something is nothing until you know a few ways to put into practice warding off the anxiety that prevents you from developing those necessary social skills.

One of the ways you can start to take the edge off of anxiety is engaging in cognitive behavioral therapy. Cognitive behavioral therapy has been proven to be incredibly beneficial to putting an end to social anxiety. The key to this type of therapy is that it is helpful in getting an individual to practice approaching the social situations that give them fear and staying in them in order to learn that, contrary to belief, nothing bad is going to happen to them and their anxiety will eventually subside. [16]

With cognitive behavioral therapy, you learn that you can overcome your anxiety and you can do it willingly to confront fear. You may also find that it is extremely empowering to conquer your fears and put yourself into situations that you would not otherwise.

Research has shown that after successful completion of cognitive behavioral therapy, people with a social anxiety disorder are in fact changed and they live a life that is no longer controlled by their fears of being put into social situations that they cannot handle. It serves to change people's thoughts, feelings, beliefs and behaviors. [16]

What is important to note as you enter cognitive behavioral therapy, is that you cannot go in with the mindset that you cannot do it. This is where a little bit of believing in yourself has to come into play. Instead of saying "I can't commit to something like this" or "My disorder is too strong for me to be able to do this, tell yourself "If I commit to this treatment, I will see results" and "I will not allow my disorder to hold me back."

There are a few simple steps you can take to implement cognitive behavioral therapy on your own before taking yourself to a therapist. [22]

- **Determine the behaviors you are avoiding**
  People with social anxiety disorder avoid anxiety-provoking situations. Are you avoiding answering

question in class? Maybe you are making an effort to keep to yourself and not speak to people at work? Or you have a family member that wants you to hang out with them and their friends but you keep putting it off? Write down all of the situations that you find yourself avoiding because of your anxiety.

- **Set up a hierarchy of fears**

Now put the fears in order from what is least likely to cause fear to most likely. It might be useful to rate them on a scale of one to 10, with one being the least anxiety-inducing and ten being the most.

- **Test your predictions**

This is useful for trying to determine how anxious you would really be in these situations as oftentimes we end up coping better than we thought we would in situations like this. Imagine yourself in each of the situations you listed and how you would react. You may even do some kind of experiment such as going out to get a coffee or food and see how you react to interacting with the cashier to gauge how you would react to other social situations.

- **Identify and eliminate safety behaviors**

Many people with anxiety engage in behaviors they think will make them feel safer in anxiety-inducing situations. These include self-medicating, holding yourself stiffly, avoiding eye contact, holding things tightly so people will not notice your hands shaking, wiping your hands so that people won't notice you are sweating and talking fast. Once you have identified your safety behaviors, make a conscious effort to stop doing them.

- **Challenge anxious thoughts**

  Another thing that people with anxiety tend to do is they will worry about how things will go well in advance of the situation. Now what you want to do is challenge those thoughts. Your mind may tell you that you are going to mess something up and you'll say back to it "Have I ever actually made a fool of myself in a situation like this though?" Argue back with your negative thoughts and do not let them win.

- **Practice doing what makes you anxious**

  The only way you will get any real experience with tackling your anxiety in confronting your fears head-on. First, you might want to start small and imagine yourself in the situations that you listed, starting with the least anxiety-inducing. Picture what exactly could happen at that moment and how you would respond. Then do some real-world exposure. Raise your hand in class. Take the initiative to start a conversation with your co-worker. Go out on a limb and take up the offer to hang out with people you don't know. All the while, push yourself to speak and interact. Understand that it is okay to be anxious in these situations and that this is all part of the learning process.

- **Practice self-reward**

  After the situation is over and you've put yourself out there, do not start criticizing everything you just did. Don't put yourself down and fret over what you could have done better. Instead, be proud of what you just did. Focus on improvements that you made and things that you did that you would never have done otherwise.

Another type of therapy that might be useful to you when it comes to edging out anxiety is group therapy.

Although a lot of individual progress can be made with individual therapy, groups are helpful in making behavioral progress. [16]

Group therapy for social anxiety involves a group comprised of only people who have a diagnosable case of social anxiety disorder. It is run by a therapist with experience in dealing with people with a social anxiety disorder and it involves specific instructions for each cognitive strategy such as introducing group members.

During the process, each strategy is explained and the therapist outlines how it will benefit your everyday life in overcoming social anxiety. The strategies are reinforced and repeated and once the strategy is learned, members of the group will practice it among each other. [16]

One strategy that is introduced during group therapy that you can easily incorporate into your own life is called slow talk. Anxiety causes a rush of adrenaline and cortisol through your system which causes you to get worked up and feel symptoms such as increased heartbeat or nausea. A lot of times when people are anxious they tend to talk fast in order to get the situation over with faster and in the process end up making the physical and mental symptoms of social anxiety even worse as they go on.

During the slow talk, you are refusing to let anxiety get you worked up and rushed. Instead, you consciously make an effort to slow down when you are speaking and regulate your nerves by reminding yourself that the situation is completely normal and nothing to be afraid of.

Some ways you can practice slow talk are speaking to yourself in a mirror before you go out and practice on others or you can read a passage from a book, all the while reminding yourself to slow down and be calm. In a group therapy setting, you would try it out on other people in the group by answering questions from other group members. [16]

There are certain changes that you can make to your everyday life to encourage you to overcome anxiety. These strategies can serve to make it easier to deal with anxiety-inducing situations as soon as you encounter them and help you to stop worrying about them in advance. Some things you can try are:

- Learn stress reduction skills
- Get exercise or physical activity on a regular basis
- Get enough sleep
- Eat a healthy, well-balanced diet
- Avoid alcohol
- Limit or avoid caffeine
- Participate in social situations with the help of people you feel comfortable around

You can also prepare for certain situations in advance. This does not mean obsessing over every detail of what you will do in a social situation like coming up with exactly what you will say, worrying about how you will stand while you talk and thinking of everything that could go wrong in that situation.

Instead, you should think about more practical ways to prepare. Instead of coming up with a script for what you will say, you can prepare for the conversation by reading up on current events or pop culture in order to have some ideas for topics you can talk about. Enhance your self-confidence by thinking of qualities that you like about yourself; people you speak to will more than likely like these things about you as well.

You can practice staying calm by practicing meditation exercises, learning stress management techniques and setting realistic goals. Shy people tend to be afraid of embarrassing themselves in social situations but think about it; how often to these embarrassing situations that you envision actually happen? Probably not often, right? And when embarrassing situations do happen, remind yourself that they do not define you and the people around you won't even remember it after a few seconds.

Once your initial treatment is over, don't just forget about it. As the saying goes, practice makes perfect. Practice the skills that you learn until they become second nature. Success comes from repetition and reinforcement of the concepts, strategies and methods, as well as their implementation, you learn throughout the process of overcoming shyness and social anxiety on a long-term basis. [16]

Reducing Fears And Insecurities Through Real-World Experiences

Before leaving the house and going out into a social situation where you will more than likely meet new people, have to introduce yourself and make conversation, you have more than likely gone through a series of anxiety-reducing strategies. After taking the courageous step of going out into a situation where you will have to socialize and confront things that trigger your social anxiety, you might be reconsidering your choice. Although fear is completely natural, there are plenty of ways to reduce your fears as you venture into real-world experiences. [22]

Studies have shown that while exposing oneself to social situations is effective in treating social anxiety, improvements with exposure alone are not as effective. Sure you can place yourself in a social situation but if you are not actively working to overcome your fears and using techniques that you practiced before entering the situation, exposure alone will not be as effective.

There are a number of social situations that you can find yourself in where you can follow a few steps before, during and afterward to work on decreasing the anxiety you feel in these situations.

These situations could be if you are going to a gathering such as a party, a wedding or a conference where you could worry about finding yourself standing alone, not sure who to talk to or how to even start a conversation. You can also find yourself in a situation a bit more small-scale such as going to lunch with a few friends or coworkers or some other kind of outing that requires you to socialize with people you don't know or don't know well. Or the situation might even be something as simple as going up to a cash register to make a purchase or going to the post office.

There are a few steps you can take before going into your social situation:[22]

- Pick an anxiety provoking situation you would like to work on. This can be a situation you have already identified as one that causes you a great amount of fear such as speaking in class or at a meeting. It can also be a situation that you cannot avoid or have put off as long as possible, such as meeting up with a friend or attending a party.
- Before going, imagine yourself in the situation. Identify the emotions you feel as you imagine it and those that you expect to feel going into it.
- Think of a rational response to those fears. For example, say you are going to go to a work meeting

and you are afraid of speaking up and voicing your opinion because you think your response will not sound intelligent and that people will not value what you say or think you are stupid because of it. The rational response would be "I know a lot about this topic, I can bring valuable insight to the conversation. There is no reason for people to not respect my opinion."

- Think about the situation and the rational response you came up with and come up with an achievable goal. In the case of the work meeting, the goal might be to speak at least once.

During the social situation, use the rational response to control the anxiety you may feel throughout. Make an effort to achieve the goal you have set. Also, aim to see the situation through to the end. If in a meeting where you are unable to leave, it may be tempting to space out so as to not have to engage. Challenge yourself to remain engaged and contribute to the conversation. If attending a gathering such as a party or a lunch, push yourself to stay until your anxiety decreases or until the situation reaches its natural end.

After the exposure to the social experience ends:[22]

- Ask yourself questions about the experience. Did you achieve your goal? How many anxiety triggers did you experience during the experience? What evidence did you gather about your rational response and how well did the rational response work?
- Summarize what you can take from the experience. What did you learn about yourself, thee particular real-world experience you were in and your response? Think of ways you can incorporate what you did into future experiences and what you can improve on.

One of the reasons that exposure might not be as effective for someone is because they are still using their safety behaviors while in the situation. These include tensing up, avoiding eye contact or self-medicating or trying to memorize what you are going to say beforehand.

Safety behaviors play an important role in actually maintaining your anxiety because they prevent people with social anxiety from experiencing confirmation of their unrealistic beliefs that they are not capable of socializing or that the people they are socializing with do not find them worthy of conversation. If safety behaviors are used, the shy person will attribute the success of the socialization to the use of their safety behaviors instead of their own merit.

Additionally, using safety behaviors can actually exacerbate physical and mental symptoms of social anxiety. For example, if you are the kind of person who attempts to control their shaking by holding their body stiffly or gripping objects, this can actually make the shaking worse and reinforce beliefs that you are not in control of your body. [22]

To consciously and effectively reduce your use of safety behaviors when you enter real-world situations, there are a few steps you can take: [22]

- First, identify situations that give you fear and the likelihood that you will encounter them.
- Identify the safety behaviors you are likely to use in each of these situations.
- Focus on disconfirming the beliefs you have in these situations, such as telling yourself that the catastrophe you expect is extremely unlikely to happy.
- Attempt to use safety behaviors as little as possible when you enter a real social situation.
- After the social situation is over, think about how well you were able to stop using safety behaviors and what you can do better next time.

Increasing Your Self-Esteem And Confidence

When it comes to shyness and social anxiety, self-esteem plays a major role. If you think little of yourself, then more than likely you will believe that others think little of you as well. Also, if you are not confident in yourself, then you will not have the courage to take risks, begin to use various therapies and skills to reduce anxiety and take the necessary steps to begin to socialize and increase your social skills.[12]

However, it is easy to tell someone will low self-esteem to just feel good about themselves. The typical advice you might hear is to just stop worrying about what other people think about you and worry about your own self-worth. You're supposed to feel better if you just think highly of yourself, right?

Well, that's easier said than done. The usual advice is to just feel better about yourself, but how do you actually get to that point? In reality, most people who struggle with self-confidence are not exactly sure what they are supposed to feel about themselves otherwise or even how to establish that positive self-image that they are told will solve all of their problems.

The first thing to keep in mind when trying to increase your self-esteem is that it is not defined by the number of accomplishments you have made. Confident people usually view themselves positively for a reason, usually having to do with the traits such as they possess such as attractiveness or intelligence or their personal achievements such as their degrees or prestigious job. [15]

While these certainly fuel confidence, they are conditional. This type of self-confidence comes from perceived individual accomplishment and possession of desirable characteristics but what is desirable for one person does not have to be for another. Another flaw in this way of thinking is that if your self-confidence comes from your accomplishments, you must keep achieving in order to feel good about yourself and when you fail at something, your self-confidence ultimately shatters.

Regardless of what one accomplishes, the feelings of accomplishments afterward are typically short-lived and they find themselves wanting to achieve more, or else they begin to feel bad about themselves again. Whether someone is are a professional sports player, a platinum award-winning singer or even the president of the United States, eventually, the thrill that comes from those accomplishments wears off and they start to get bored. If people constantly have to achieve to feel self-confidence, they will find themselves in an endless cycle of trying to achieve more but never quite feeling satisfied. [15]

Another fleeting source of self-esteem comes from good behaviors. Good deeds can fuel a person's self-confidence because they believe that because they are helping someone this makes them a good person. While this is true and doing good deeds are a great way to help others, if one is basing their value as a person entirely around good behavior, they fall into the same trap as someone who bases their self-esteem on their accomplishments.

People believe that they achieve something, it will eradicate feelings of inadequacy but in reality, a truly permanent source of self-esteem comes from something else. No external factor is going to give you the self-confidence that you desire. Instead of basing your self-confidence on achievements, behaviors or personal attractiveness, it should come from within.

Instead, think of characteristics that you like about yourself, things that make you a good person. These would be your personality, your kindness, your smile. Do you have a good sense of humor? Are you very knowledgeable about a certain topic? Start by coming up with good traits that you have and remind yourself that these are something to be proud of and you can always set goals to improve on them. [15]

With low self-confidence, people tend to doubt their abilities. They don't believe they can accomplish difficult tasks and will crumble in the face of failure. Because of this, they shy away from difficult tasks in the favor of comfort but end up not moving forward in life into new experiences and opportunities because they do not believe they can.

Another factor that will help to build your self-esteem is your amount of self-efficacy. Self-efficacy is so important because it determines how people feel, think, behave and motivate themselves as well as increases personal well-being and accomplishment. Ultimately, the more self-efficacy you have, the better you will feel about yourself. You will have higher assurance in your capabilities and will not let failure debilitate your personal growth.

There are a few ways you can increase your own sense of self-efficacy: [12]

- **Mastery experiences**
Overcoming obstacles and achieving personal goals, is a great way to build one's personal self-efficacy. However, these shouldn't just be easy accomplishments, otherwise, you will come to believe that it comes from quick results and you may become easily discouraged by failure. Resilience comes from

overcoming difficult obstacles and in order to succeed in these, it is time to take some risks that you would not normally take on and see what happens. This can be as simple as saying hello to a stranger while you are out one day or as complex as going to a party and interacting with tons of people that you don't know very well.

Whatever you have laid out as your most intense fears, facing them head-on will certainly build a strong sense of self-efficacy for you. If you experience difficulties in these risks, do not give up. Sometimes setbacks have to happen before people can accomplish their goals. It all requires a sustained effort. However, when people are able to meet their goals, they begin to realize that it is possible to succeed and it becomes easier in the long run.

- **Social models**
Seeing people similar to you succeed in things that you want to accomplish can give you a sense that it is possible. These can be people that have the same goals as you or people who have similar

characteristics as you. Maybe you relate to a person because they have a similar personality or they struggle with the same difficulties with shyness, social anxiety or low self-confidence. These people can be someone you know in person or someone you know from a distance like a celebrity or an online influencer like a blogger. It helps the more similar a person is to you because their successes and failures are more persuasive. From seeing them succeed, you see that it is possible to possess the capabilities required to accomplish your personal goals.

At the same time, seeing others fail at things you are trying to succeed in can actually serve to encourage you as you see that you do not need to set yourself too high standards and you understand that it can happen to anyone. Through their actions, these models set an example for you through their behavior and expressed way of thinking and teach through the skills that they demonstrate.

- **Social persuasion**

This can come about through verbal persuasion through a friend, family member or an acquaintance. Being around others who are more outgoing and vocal often helps one who is shy feel as though this is something that they can do. People who are persuaded verbally that they do in fact possess the capabilities to socialize and master given activities are more likely to sustain their efforts to be more outgoing than if they have self-doubts or dwell on personal deficiencies when problems arise along the way.

However, if you are easily persuaded verbally, it is important to ensure that you are not swayed by negative social persuasion such as being told that you lack the capabilities to take on difficult tasks. If so, it may even more possible that you give up easily in the face of difficulty. Whatever persuasion you receive from others, make sure that you are regularly persuading yourself to put yourself out there and know that you are capable on your own.

- **Reduce stress reactions**

A lot of times, people rely on their somatic and emotional states to get through situations and judge their capabilities in such situations. Therefore, they interpret stress reactions as a sign of vulnerability or incapability. Mood also affects the judgement of how good you are and how well you will do. Find ways to reduce stress such as meditation, exercise and getting enough sleep as well as maintain a positive attitude. It will benefit your sense of self-efficacy and self-esteem and because of that boost your social skills.

Why Can Your Confidence And Social Skills Fluctuate So Much?

While in the process of overcoming social anxiety, it is possible for you to have moments of great confidence and accomplishment, as well as setbacks.

What is important to understand when tackling the issue of shyness and social anxiety, is that it did not begin overnight. These are habits and mindsets that you have built over many years, probably since early childhood. So you are not going to be able to completely reduce these problems in one day, let alone in one sitting.

Through the skills and strategies, you acquire through this process, as well as the therapies and treatments you may attend to further your journey, you will have times where you make a lot of progress. There will be moments of triumph where you make a new friend, you make eye contact with a stranger while having a conversation, you are able to stop using your safety behaviors and you are comfortable giving a presentation in class.

However, there will also be moments in between where you are back to square one. You may find yourself leaving a gathering very early for fear of having to interact with people you do not know very well while just the day before you struck up a decent conversation with a stranger at your friend's birthday party on your own. There will be times where you think that you have left your shyness in the past but you wake up one day feeling less confident and not sure if you want to go to the movies with your friends after all.

Sometimes these things will happen because you are still learning and you are still making this newfound self-confidence and social skills a habit and a commitment. As with anything, setbacks are completely normal and should not discourage you or deter you from continuing to make progress.

An important step to take, not only when you find yourself in a setback situation but throughout the entire process of moving on from shyness, is acceptance. This is not so much accepting that this is how you are and will always be so to discourage yourself from changing at all. But acceptance is a way of looking at ourselves, as well as the world, and implies a willingness and openness to seeing things as they really are without any judgment. [14]

This means that if you are feeling anxious, even after experiences success in overcoming your anxiety, it's okay. This does not mean that you are going to completely revert back to your old ways and never be able to overcome your shyness for good. Acceptance does not mean that social anxiety will last forever and it does not mean that you will not be able to handle it. This just means that you are feeling anxious in the moment and that is okay.

A few things to keep in mind about acceptance are, for one thing, that it does not equal approval. Accepting the fact that you are shy does not mean that you approve of it and that you wish to remain shy. It also does not mean that you are giving up and does not preclude taking appropriate action. Recognizing that you are shy and experiencing symptoms of social anxiety does not mean that you will not use various coping skills and strategies to overcome it. But it means that you are paying attention and plan to take appropriate action. [14]

Overall, acceptance alleviates unnecessary suffering. Certainly, you will feel pain at some point, you might have some of those setbacks towards your progress, but acceptance can lead to having peace amongst these experiences. Acceptance is not something that comes quickly or easily, there will definitely moments where you do not want to accept that this is happening and you just want to snap your fingers and make it go away.

Acceptance is a process, similar to that of the grieving process. When experiencing a fluctuation of confidence and social skills, think of it as going through a few different steps: shock that you have reverted back to a previous mindset or action that you thought you were over, denial that this is possible, anger that you allowed this to happen and didn't stick to the techniques that you had laid out and had been working so well, despair that you have fallen back into step with old behaviors unsure if you can come out of it and finally acceptance.[14]

When you experience a fluctuation in your confidence and social skills, there are a few steps you can take to not let it get the best of you: [14]

- **Recognize the non-affirming thought**

  Suppose you are at a convention, an immense accomplishment for you after your previous history with avoiding crowded places like the plague. You are proud of yourself for coming out with a few friends and see it as the most important step you have taken in this journey to overcome shyness. While there, you find yourself standing next to a stranger who strikes up a conversation but you suddenly become nervous, stumble over your words and out of fear for humiliating yourself further you run off.

  Before you can move on, you must recognize that you are having this thought and make moves to address it. Acknowledge this as a slip-up and think of the thoughts that ran through your mind at that moment which caused you to get so nervous.

- **Apologize to yourself**

Do not beat yourself up and berate yourself for having this one slip up. This is important because you do not want to fall into the trap of putting yourself down; you don't speak to other people so cruelly so why should you do it to yourself? You had one moment of weakness. That should not undermine all of the progress you have made up to this point.

- **Question the validity of the thought**

  Examine the evidence of the statement you made to yourself that caused you to get nervous at that moment. What is the evidence that statement is true? Who says it is true? Who gives them the right to decide that is true? Does it really matter if it is true or not? More than likely it does not matter and there is no evidence that it is true at all.

- **Replace the thought with an affirmation**

  Give yourself a positive, more self-accepting thought to leave that situation with. These can be anything along the lines of "I accept myself," "I have many gifts to offer the world" or "If I accept myself, it won't matter what other people think." Remind yourself that you have worked hard up to this point and one fluctuation will not undo the progress that you have made.

Social Skills

Are Social Skills Genetic?

Some studies have suggested that some characteristics that only humans possess, such as empathy, altruism, sense of equity, love, trust, music, economic behavior and politics, are partially ingrained into our system.[11]

There are a few genes, such as the arginine vasopressin receptor and the oxytocin receptor, that contribute to social behavior in a lot of different species, which includes humans. These are two of the most-studied brain signaling molecules that serve to encode information relevant to social behavior. They play a key role in indicating social interactions. Other polymorphic genes, such as those encoding for dopamine reward pathways and serotonergic emotional regulation further enable human social behaviors.[11]

However, with some people having more difficulties than others when it comes to this essential rule of life, scientist have set out to discover why although learning about mental illness presents more of a challenge than studying other types of illness considering the complexity of the human brain.

Twin studies have been essential in the discovery of the genetic factors that play a role in social behavior and sure enough, they have found that genes play a role in our ability to understand and manipulate social relationships. [11]

These twin studies have shown that although twins can be were raised in the exact same family environment and have had the same influences on them throughout their early life, they can develop different social tendencies due to the differences in their genetic makeup.

Twin studies have also shown that 52 to 72 percent of adult twins possessed inheritable traits such as altruism, empathy and nurturance without much attribution to their environment growing up. Consistent patterns also showed that genetics and non-shared environments become more important past childhood. [11]

Another study showed that genetics play a part in social skills from the ages of 11 to 17, critical years of development where people are making friends, interacting and looking for acceptance on a regular basis. It is natural that social behavior changes over the course of development and the genetics that go along with it change as well.

The study suggested that that genetic influence over social skills comes into play after puberty and wane throughout the next several years. These genetic factors that cause social difficulties are different than those that cause autism or schizophrenia as those with autism develop at a younger age while with schizophrenics, these factors reach their culmination at the age of at least 17.

This hinted at a new genetic factor contributing to communication skills. By age 11, different genetic factors come into play that affects social skills and they have more of an effect as people go through their adolescent years. [8]

Genetic vulnerability plays a role in social behaviors such as empathy where genetics have been shown to account for change and continuity in empathy as children grew up, as well as social stress and aggression where developmental genes determine response to stress.

If you suffer from any level of shyness or social anxiety, it is likely that there is some level of genetic factors that play a role in your possession of social skills. While it is not really much you can do about the genes themselves, you can have some level of control over it by changing the way you respond to these involuntary factors.[8]

Three Styles Of Communication With Other People

If you are ever out alone, or even with people you are close to, take some time to observe the way people communicate. Try to pinpoint people who are loud and boisterous, quiet or insistent.Naturally, people communicate with each other in different ways but there are three distinct communication styles people use; aggressive, submissive and assertive.

People who use the aggressive communication style often fall into the mindset of "Everyone should be like me" and "I am never wrong." This communication style tends to be closed-minded and because of this, people who are aggressive communicators tend to be poor listeners and have difficulty seeing another [18] person's point of view. They often interrupt and monopolize the conversation.

The aggressive communicator likes to achieve their goals, but unfortunately, this is usually at the expense of another person. They tend to be domineering, condescending as well as patronizing and will bully others. It is easy to pick them out by their behavior as they will often put others down and are bossy, don't show appreciation and they don't ever think they are wrong. They often try to overpower others, especially those weaker than them and have a know-it-all attitude. [18]

There are a few nonverbal and verbal cues that distinguish them. Nonverbally, they will point, frown, squint their eyes critically, glare, have a rigid posture, and use a critical, loud or yelling tone of voice. They might use a lot of verbal abuse and say things like "Don't ask why, just do it" or "You must do this."

They solve their problems by winning arguments, often using threats or attacks, and they operate from a win/lose position. They usually feel some level of anger, hostility, frustration and impatience. [18]

They end up provoking arguments from others and end up alienating themselves from the rest of the crowd. They end up wasting time trying to supervise others and from fostering resistance, defiance, sabotaging, striking back, forming alliances, lying and covering up; they pay the price of having meaningful relationships with other people.

Keep in mind that not all aggressive communicators are negative. There are actually a few advantages of using an aggressive communication style. For one thing, they make great leaders because they feel comfortable leading a conversation or speaking for most of the time and command respect from the people around them. [10]

They have a strong voice and they make sure their voice is heard as are not afraid to be heard over others. They also tend to not show vulnerability and maintain superiority in most dynamic relationships.

Next, there is the passive communication style. While the aggressive communicator is loud and has no problem saying what is on their mind and pushing others out of the way, the passive communicator acts indifferently, often yielding to others. They usually fail to express their feelings or needs and instead allow others to express themselves. Their lack of outward communication can lead to misunderstanding, anger build-up or resentment.[18]

Someone with a passive communication style believes it is not necessary to express their true feelings or disagree and they might often think that others have more rights to do so than them. Their communication style in indirect, hesitant and they always agree and don't speak up.

Passive communicators will be self-conscious and apologetic, usually trusting others more than themselves. They allow others to make decisions for them, they don't express their own wants and feelings and they don't get what they need or want. They sigh a lot, try to sit on both sides to avoid conflict, ask permission unnecessarily and complain instead of taking action. They have difficulty implementing plans and are self-effacing. [18]

Nonverbally, you would see a passive communicator fidget a lot, have downcast eyes, smile and nod in agreement, have a lot volume, and speak fast when they are anxious and slowly when unsure. They come across as pleading and lack facial animation. You might hear them say that someone else should do it and say others have more experience than them as well as say things like "I can't" or "I'll try." They usually speak in a low, monotone voice.

Usually, they feel powerless and wonder why they don't receive credit for their work which they chalk up to other's abilities. This leads them to do things like give up on themselves and build dependency on relationships. They don't know where they stand and lose their self-esteem.

But like the aggressive communication style, there are some positives to the passive communication style. For one thing, they are thoughtful and make sure the needs of others are met. They go with the flow and let others lead but they are easy to get along with. Unfortunately, people tend to take advantage of them but they like to avoid conflicts. [10]

Finally, there is the assertive communication style. Those who use the assertive communication style believe themselves and other people are valuable. They understand that that assertiveness doesn't mean you always win, but that you handled the situation as effectively as possible. The motto they live by is "I have rights and so do others." [18]

Their communication style is effective because they are active listeners but they state their limits and expectations as well as their observations. They don't judge. They express themselves directly, honestly, and as soon as possible about feelings and wants but they also check in on others feelings.

Assertive communicators are observers rather than labelers who trust themselves and others and are confident. They are self-aware, open, flexible, versatile as well as playful in their sense of humor, decisive and proactive. They operate by choice and know what is needed and develop a plan to get it. They are action-oriented, firm and realistic in their expectations. Additionally, they are fair and consistent and they take appropriate action toward getting what she wants without denying rights of others. [18]

When you communicate with the assertive communicator, you will find them using open and natural gestures with an interesting facial expression. They use direct eye-contact, have a confident and relaxed posture, and use an appropriate and natural vocal volume and rate of speech. They say things like "I choose to," "What are my options?" and "What alternatives do we have?"

When confronting their problems, they are able to negotiate, bargain, tradeoff and compromise. They confront problems as they happen and don't let negative feelings build up. They go into situations with enthusiasm and are even-tempered. They have an increased self-esteem and self-confidence and increase the self-esteem of others, they feel motivated and understood and others know where they stand.

Additionally, they do not fear or avoid conflict. They are level headed about things and tend to not let emotions get the best of them in high conflict situations. They can distinguish between fact and opinion and share their vulnerabilities. They aim for both sides to win in a situation, balancing one's rights with the rights of others.[10]

The question is which communication style do you currently use and which one should you strive for? Ultimately, good communication skills require a certain level of self-awareness and by deciding which communication style you should use is essential to determine not only how you will communicate with others, but how others will perceive you.

In most situations, you would want to aim for the assertive communication style to interact with others in a well-balanced and inclusive way. However, the other styles of communication can be essential at certain times as well.

A few times where you can use the assertive communication style are:[18]

- when a decision has to be made quickly;
- during emergencies;
- when you know you're right and that fact is crucial;
- when you can stimulate creativity by designing competitions destined for use in training or to increase productivity.

And you can use the passive communication style when: [18]

- when an issue is minor;
- when the problems caused by the conflict are greater than the conflict itself;
- when emotions are running high and it makes sense to take a break in order to calm down and regain perspective;

- when your power is much lower than the other party's;
- when the other's position is impossible to change for all practical purposes (i.e., government policies, etc.).

Use your own judgement in each situation that you find yourself in to determine which communication style you will use.

How To Open/Start A Conversation

Going out into a social situation takes courage. For getting to that point, you should commend yourself for putting yourself out there. However, once you get there and you come face to face with a stranger or a person you do not know very well, things can get awkward very fast unless you know how to begin a conversation.

Being shy can be awkward enough, but starting a conversation adds a whole new layer to the fears that social anxiety can give you. Despite the initial intimidation, starting a conversation does not have to be as awkward as you may think.

When you approach a stranger, when a stranger approaches you or when the conversation you're having start to wear thin and awkward silences follow, there are a few different approaches you can take to starting a conversation. [24]

- **Invitations**

  These are questions that you use to get the conversation started. There are a number of things you can ask about such as about the social situation you are in, you can ask about mutual friends or you can ask about what they think of current events or pop culture. If it comes down to it you can even ask about the weather. It's a basic conversation topic but it is something everyone experiences and if you are running out of ideas, the weather is a good place to start.

- **Inspirations**

  Here you take inspiration from your own life by telling the person you are talking to about something you have experienced. This opens the conversation up for your partner to comment on or ask more questions about the story you tell. Do you have an interesting childhood story you can tell? Maybe something funny happened to you last week that you would like to share? Better yet, if you've had previous experience with the situation you are in, bring it up.

Say for example your friend is having a house party and there are a lot of people there that you don't know very well. You end up talking to someone and after exchanging names and the usual "how are you?" you tell them about the fun time you had at your friend's last party or any other specific story you have that relates to this place. This will leave an opening for the person you are talking with to ask questions and prompt them to tell a story that they have with your friends. Conversations like this can go on for a long time and chances are you might find out something in common that you have with this person and things you can relate to. Soon you will find that the conversation flows effortlessly and your worries about starting the conversation will be long forgotten.

- **Observations**

Take a look at something around you and use it to start a conversation. This means asking a sincere question about the situation you are in, spontaneous questions that pop into your head about where you are. For example, if you are on a train you can ask if they serve snacks on the train. If they respond positively with a "Yes, I think they do," then you can follow up with something like "Do you take this train often?" As another example, say you are sitting in class next to someone you don't know well. There are lots of questions here that can relate to the professor, the assignments and more. One thing you can say is "Did you read the assignment for today?" If they say yes, you can follow up by asking them what they thought of it. Even if they say no, you can tell them what you thought of it.

Like invitations, observations can open the door to a more in-depth conversation. It may seem simple to start out with just a thought about the environment you are in, with the proper introduction; these can turn into conversations where you learn a lot about another person.

- **Positive remarks**

  These involve making a positive statement about the situation you're in or the people you are around. Suppose you are at a coffee shop one morning. You are the only person in line and you are face-to-face with the cashier. A few minutes remain until your drink is ready. Instead of standing there awkwardly, take a look around the room and make a positive remark to spark conversation. Mention how you cute the new cup designs are, how the song playing is one of your favorites or say how nice the new decor in the shop is.

The key here is that you are not making a positive remark about the person you are talking to. This is more of an extension of the observations strategy.

However, positive remarks signal to the person you are talking to that you are easy to make conversation with that you are a kind and positive person.

- **Get to know**

These are questions that you can ask people to get to know them better in situations such as at school, at work or a dinner party. Take, for example, there is a new person at your job and you want to get to know them to make them feel comfortable. There are endless questions you can ask to get to know them such as "Where are you from?" "How long have you been doing this?" "What was your last position like?" Whatever the person's response is, stay on that same topic and ask a follow-up position. If they say they are from a different city or state, you can ask "What brings you here?"

Unlike positive remarks, the key here is that you are going to be asking questions about them. This works better in situations such as parties, starting a new job or some other gathering where you will likely be interacting with a person for a more extended period of time than just a few minutes while getting an order from a store. After the person answers your question, ask follow up questions until that topic reaches its natural end then you can change topics, still asking about them. This method shows that you are taking interest in that person which they will appreciate and more than likely reciprocate.

- **Relate to a previous conversation**

You won't always be in situations with strangers. Sometimes you will be talking to a friend, or at least someone you know well, and don't know what to say. One of the solutions, in this case, can be talking about a previous conversation. Say you are going to see a movie with a friend and you need to start a new conversation topic. You remember weeks ago when your friend asked you to come to the movie and how they talked about how much they loved the action in the first movie of the series. You can relate back to that conversation by saying something like "Hey, I remember you saying you liked this scene from the first movie. What do you think will happen in this one?" More than likely your friend will be excited to talk about the movie more in depth and they will be happy that you remembered what they said before.

This method can help to strengthen friendships because it shows people that you listen to them and genuinely care about them. Your friends get the idea that you have taken an interest in their interest or what they say and they will be more likely to take an interest in your interests as well.

You can start a conversation by either asking a question or making a statement. Usually, questions are easier when you're just starting to build your social skills because they require the other person to answer, but statements are just as effective when you need to open a conversation. After all, normal conversations are a mix of questions and statements.

Whether you decide to use a question or a statement in a conversation, the goal overall is to keep the conversation going by enticing the other person to speak and give you more information to work with.

How To Talk To People On A Personal Level And Make It Past A Thirty-Second Conversation

Despite memorizing a few questions and being able to observe your surroundings and form a conversation topic based on that, sometimes it can still be difficult to keep a conversation going, especially with someone you do not know very well.

Imagine a situation where you are at some kind of gathering, a work meeting or a seminar or something like that, where you are obligated to speak to people. There you find yourself face to face with someone you don't know well and who do not have any common interests with you. A situation like that can get awkward really fast and it can be really hard to keep a conversation going until it just falls apart completely.

Fortunately, there are a few ways you can engage someone in a conversation and not just a shallow, 30-second conversation where you don't learn anything about the other person. Instead, you can take a conversation to a personal level by understanding the person you are speaking to and taking a few steps to build up to a conversation.

When engaging a person in a conversation, seek to understand the person you are talking to and incorporate that into the way you speak to them. This means understanding what kind of communication style they use. If they have a strong personality and use the aggressive communication style, try to be more outgoing so as to not bore them. If they are more of a passive communicator, try not to be too loud or overbearing so as to not overwhelm them.

Another thing to keep in mind when trying to understand the person you are talking to understands the difference in communication styles between women and men. There are of course exceptions to every rule, but generally, men are much better at public speaking while women are better at private speaking. [23]

For women, this means establishing connections and negotiating relationships placing emphasis on displaying similarities and matching experiences. Meanwhile, for men, their communication habits revolve around preserving the independence and negotiating and maintaining status in social order. To do this, they try to exhibit knowledge and skill.

The key to successfully engaging a person you don't know well in conversation lies in finding common ground with the person you are communicating with and using the right amount of personal disclosure, empathy and tact. This means finding a good balance between talking about yourself, and not overwhelming the conversation with just facts about you. Ensure that you are giving the other person enough room to speak so that you can learn about them and move the conversation along. [23]

Overall, there are a few things to keep in mind when trying to engage a person in a deeper conversation:

- **Listen**

This is one of the most important things you can do when trying to hold a deep conversation with someone. For one thing, it is a sign of respect. So if you show the person you are speaking to that you are actively listening to them by not simply listening but displaying with your body language (attentive posture, making eye contact) that you are listening, this not only makes them more likely to listen to you but it makes them feel heard and respected and they will want to continue to carry on a conversation with you.

Listening also serves another purpose. Ensure that you are actively listening to what the person is saying because you can follow up on their words to continue on the conversation. Suppose they are talking about where they grew up and how the city or town means a lot to them even to this day. You might follow up by asking why it meant so much to them or what they learned from it. By actively listening, you can determine not only what the person is saying that you can play off of, but you can get an idea of how they feel about what they're talking about. Listen to what evokes a strong reaction out of the person you are speaking to and use those points to further the conversation.

- **Reflect**

  Listening is important to this step because when someone tells you something, a great way to continue on with the conversation is to restate what you heard or what you think you heard. This doesn't really mean repeating the person word for word. Suppose you are talking with them about music and they say "My favorite band is Aerosmith. I really like rock music." You can respond with "Oh, so you like classic rock?"

  This can prompt them to clarify the type of rock music they like and expand on more of their favorite bands and songs. Reflecting is another way to show that you are listening and it will make the other person feel valued in the conversation. It also gives them a chance to clarify their words for you.

- **Read body language**

This serves a few purposes when it comes to carrying on a conversation. Much like listening to their tone of voice, the body language shows what a person feels strongly about which are points you can comment on as you continue your conversation. Maybe the person gets excited and starts using elaborate hand gestures when they talk about something that means a lot to them or that makes them happy. Maybe they cross their arms or furrow their brow when they start discussing something that is a source of great annoyance to them.

Not only does reading body language give clues to how they feel about what they are talking about, it gives you an idea of how they feel about the conversation as well. If they are making eyes contact, are sitting up straight or are leaning towards you, it is likely that they are very engaged in the conversation and enjoy speaking to you. However, if they start leaning away, hunching over or looking at something else, you can infer that the conversation is not satisfying to them. If it begins to look like the person you are talking to is not engaged with the conversation anymore it may be time to change topics. Or maybe the conversation has reached an end and that's okay too. Don't see it as a failure but an opportunity that you took advantage of. Think of what you did well and what you could do differently for the next one.

- **Know when not to talk**

  After initiating a conversation, you are inclined to carry on the conversation by asking questions and providing your own input. However, ensuring that the person you are having a conversation with is able to get a word it is very important to have a meaningful conversation. When you are nervous about having a conversation, especially when you are just starting to polish your social skills, you might tend to ramble unintentionally.

  Coming to a natural end with your responses will become easier the more you talk to people, but until then if you are the type of person to ramble out of nervousness attempt to limit your responses to no more than a few sentences. This gives the other person a chance to get a word in and does not turn them off to the conversation entirely.

How To Engage Someone In A Conversation

Equipped with the tools needed to start a conversation, the only thing that remains is to just do it. The more you socialize and have conversations with people you know and people that you don't know; you will start to become more comfortable with engaging people in conversations. It will soon be second nature.

Until then, it could be useful to have a set list of steps that you follow when you go into social interactions. When anxiety starts to take hold of people, it is easy for your mind to get scrambled and forget what you should say next. Memorizing a few steps that you can follow as you interact with people and engage them in conversation will provide a little bit of a cushion to fall back on when you find yourself getting nervous as you socialize.

- **Accept your anxiety and act through it**

  Even though you've made the decision to go out and socialize, you will more than likely experience symptoms of anxiety before you start to engage in conversation with others. Rapid heart rate, sweating, shaking, apprehension; all symptoms that you have more than likely experienced before. However, instead of letting the anxiety stop you from socializing and letting it convince you to turn around and go home to your safe space, accept it. Accept that this is what you are experiencing at this moment, but make the commitment to work through it and do not let it control you.

  Even if you are in the middle of the conversation and things start to wane, you might feel a sense of panic and all of these feelings start rushing back. No matter what, acceptance is the way to go because believe it or not, acceptance actually can take some of the edge off. Think positive thoughts before, during and after the conversation. Say to yourself "I can do this" and "There is no reason to panic." The anxiety may not go away completely, but fighting it only serves to make it worse because you end up fueling it by thinking about it so much.

Don't be ashamed of how you feel. Instead, change your perspective to be more realistic. A lot of shy people have irrational and illogical beliefs about how a conversation will go. It ultimately makes you more nervous and inhibits you from making the most of the conversation. Instead of focusing on our inadequacies, focus on what you can do. Understand that everyone has some level of self-doubt and are going through their own struggles. Tell yourself that you are doing your best and putting yourself out there to speak to others is an accomplishment in itself.

- **Exchange formalities**
  It's a basic step in the process and can seem tedious but it is necessary to ease into the conversation instead of jumping straight into asking about the person's life goals. Shake hands, introduce yourself and exchange a "How are you?" Even ask them a

question about the environment you are in. If your mutual friend is throwing a party, you can say "How do you know (person's name)?" If you are at a work meeting, you can ask "What department do you work for?" Or if you are at some other kind of gathering or party you can say "What brings you here?" Getting to know the person on a name basis and finding out basic information about them is the first step to moving into a more in-depth conversation.

- **Be observant**

Here you can start bringing in broad conversation topics. At this point, you don't know much about them on a personal level, but you can ask broad questions to get a sense of the kind of things they enjoy and what their personality is like. This is where techniques like observations and positive remarks come in. If you are at a party, you can comment on the music that is playing and say something like "I really like this song" or "This artists' last album was really great." If you are at a dinner party you can comment on the food. Suppose you are at a cookout at a park, you can mention how the scenery with the trees and the lake are really beautiful.

These open up the floor for the other person to respond with something that you can follow up on. For example, at the party, they might respond with "That album was my favorite!" or "I liked the last one better." It leaves an easy way for you to follow up by simply asking why which will get them to speak more. Then you can find more topics to follow up on and continue the pattern for a little while. In the early phase of a conversation, looking around you for anything that might be worth commenting on is a definite way to get a conversation started.

- **Start getting personal**

  Now that you have exchanged names and formalities with the person and started with basic conversation topics, this is when you can get deeper and really engage them. By now you have probably learned something about them such as their favorite music, their favorite food or where they work. You've also got an idea of their personality and what kind of communication style they follow. There are endless turns the conversation can take from here. You can start asking personal questions like where they are from, things that are important to them or their favorite books and movies. Or you can ask what they think about topics that are currently in the news. Even find out how they feel about the event you are attending, this is especially easy if you are at some kind of book or movie convention or a theme park.

- **Use their responses to keep the conversation going and share some of yourself**

  Up to this point, you have successfully gotten to know a person and started a pretty engaging conversation. Now you just have to keep the conversation going. Sometimes the conversation may start to dwindle and when that happens things can get a little nerve-racking. But keep in mind as you start to throw out more topics to see what sticks, it's not always going to be the first thing you say that ends up being important, but their response. They might say something unexpected that you can follow up with and continue the conversation in that direction.

As an example, suppose you end up talking about books. You say "What do you think of fantasy novels?" in an attempt to keep your conversation going. At that moment they perk up and go "I love fantasy! Do you read J. R. R. Tolkien? I love Lord of the Rings." Going off of that response, you proceed to ask them about Lord of the Rings. By using this method, it is easier to get a fun topic out of a mundane one.

But don't be afraid to share a little about yourself as well. Don't overwhelm the conversation and don't overshare, but get a feel for a natural balance of learning about the other person and sharing information about yourself. Opening up about your thoughts can be scary as a shy person. It's much easier to just ask questions and let the other person speak. However, when the conversation does start to wane and the person you are speaking to is running out of things to say, it's time to flip the script and share something about yourself to give them a chance to ask follow up questions.

By revealing yourself, you build a connection with that person. It's not just a one-sided conversation with only them sharing information about themselves. If both of you begin to feel like you know each other, that's when the conversation starts to flow naturally and you will find that you don't actually have to think so hard about what to say next and how to keep things moving.

Asking Questions In Conversations To Get To Know Each Other Better

Imagine being at a party talking to a stranger. You have followed through the steps to having a conversation. You have now successfully introduced yourself to a person you don't know and moved past basic conversation tactics to get to know the person in a deep, interesting conversation.

But suddenly, the conversation starts to fall away. You have both exhausted the topic that had led to such an easy flow between the two of you. The person is starting to look uncomfortable or uninterested and you are starting to panic. You don't know what to say next to keep the conversation going.

This is one of the fears of many shy or socially anxious people as they begin socializing and testing out their social skills. Talking to others and exposing yourself to people and situations you wouldn't dream of encountering otherwise is nice and all, but what do you do when you can't think of anything else to ask?

Here are a few examples of questions you can ask to not only keep the conversation going but get to know people better. Whether it is a stranger or a person you know fairly well, certain questions are sure to spark an interesting dialogue between the two of you and create more of a connection.

1. What are you currently working on that has you the most excited?

2. If money were no longer an issue - what would you be doing with your life?

3. What is your favorite charity?

4. What are your long-term and short-term goals?

5. If you could travel anywhere, where would you go?

6. Who has been the most influential person in your life?

7. What is your all-time favorite book?

8. Where are you from and what influence did it have on you growing up?

9. What is your favorite thing to do in your free time?

10. What is the most important lesson you have learned in life?

Try to memorize a list of questions like this. That way, when you go into a social situation and nervousness starts to creep up on you or the conversation is simply beginning to lose momentum, you don't have to frantically search your mind for something interesting to say.

What Not To Do In Conversations: The Don'ts

Don't Judge

This is incredibly important when you are starting a conversation with someone new. For one thing, if you start judging someone in the very beginning of the conversation, or before you even start talking, you form for yourself predetermined expectations of that person which can be detrimental to the conversation. Suppose you approach someone at a work meeting. He's a clean-cut businessman and doesn't smile very much. If you determine before you even start talking that he's rigid, rude or won't be willing to open up, you will speak to him and direct the conversation based off those expectations. You might speak to him a bit harsher and be less open when it turns out he is, in fact, a much laid back person with a funny personality but also needed some help coming out of his shell.

More often than not, people can sense when someone is judging them unfairly. If a person feels judged by you, they will be less likely to want to open up to you which can cause the conversation to fall apart. So keep an open mind when you are talking to someone and reserve your judgment about the person until the conversation is over.

Don't Overshare

Avoid telling strangers your most private secrets for a few reasons. For one thing, that information can spread amongst others to people you don't necessarily want to know. Suppose this person is friends with someone else you know. Whether it is someone you know well or not, you may not want many people to know that information about you. Another thing is people tend to feel uncomfortable when they hear a stranger's deepest secrets. Knowing about things like the family disputes, medical conditions and love affairs of others, people may feel uncomfortable because they feel like they are intruding or they don't really know how to respond. This can easily derail a conversation. Finally, oversharing can make you a bore. Other's don't want to hear it and in face-to-face interaction, walking away can be difficult.

Don't Interrupt

One sure way to derail a conversation is to interrupt the other person. And sometimes interrupting can't be helped. You might find yourself in a situation where the other person takes a pause and you think they are done but they continue just as you're starting to say something. That's fine, but keep those instances very minimal. As your conversation goes on, you might find a topic that you enjoy and sometimes when we get excited about something, that leads us to interrupt so we can get out point across sooner. Try to avoid this altogether. Let the other person finish their thought completely instead of cutting them off. The more you interrupt, the more annoyed the other person will become and inevitably they will feel like you don't respect them in the conversation or you are not interested in what they have to say.

Don't Give Too Short Answers

When a person is shy it is much easier to ask questions and let the other person do most of the talking. But they expect to hear from you just as much. Avoid giving one-word answers or answers that are too short. You expect to be able to follow up on answers the other person gives with more questions and they expect to do the same. Thoughtful answers will help move the conversation along because between the two of you there will be more to talk about. Also, when you give thoughtful answers, the person you are speaking to will feel that you are engaged in the conversation as well. Otherwise, they may feel like you are not enjoying the conversation and don't want to talk in the first place.

Don't Monopolize The Conversation

Even though you want to make sure you are not giving one-word answers, you also want to ensure that you are not overwhelming the conversation. If you're giving incredibly long answers and dominating the conversation, this has the same effect as you not giving answers that are long enough. It serves to make your conversation partner uninterested by making them feel like you are not interested in anything that they say. If you are going to dominate the conversation, you might as well be talking to yourself. Find a balance between asking questions and giving the other person enough time to speak, but letting yourself have enough input to keep the conversation moving along naturally.

Don't Change Topics Too Quickly

As you are socializing you want to keep the conversation going by asking questions and learning more about the person you are speaking to. However, hanging topics too quickly is another definite way to ensure that the conversation does not go as smoothly as you want it to. Suppose you both become engaged in a topic that the other persons seems to be very interested in, but suddenly you ask a completely different question in the middle of it. There might come a time where you end up talking about something that you are not particularly interested in, and that is fine, but changing the topics too fast makes it obvious. Let the other person say their piece about the topic and try to find a natural end to it before you change the subject. It will make for less awkwardness in the long run and make your conversation partner want to keep speaking to you.

Putting It In Practice

The 10-Day Challenge To Improve Social Skills

Day 1: Determine Your Fear

Confronting your fears from a personal standpoint can be difficult, intimidating even. But the first thing you want to do is lay out your fears in front of your own eyes with the intention of confronting them. Confrontation and risk-taking are what this process is all about.

The first thing you want to do in this process is simply writing a list of what causes you fear when you think of socializing. These can include experiencing anxiety symptoms (quick heartbeat, shaking, sweating), stumbling over your words, looking visibly afraid, embarrassing yourself, making the other person think you are unintelligent. Whatever it is, don't be scared to write it down.

Along with those fears, create a list of social situations that cause you anxiety. These can be anything from speaking in front of others (whether in a small group or a public speaking setting), ordering from a restaurant to talking to strangers at a social gathering. Once you have a list of situations that cause you anxiety, set up a hierarchy by ordering them from least intimidating to most intimidating. This will make it easier to choose what to start exposing yourself to at a later date.

Finally, start a journal of your feelings. This can be really helpful in tracking your progress over the course of lessening your social anxiety. Start on the first day by just jotting down some of the emotions you are feeling at the thought of embarking on this journey. Some of that may be fear, and some of it may even be excitement at the idea of finally putting an end to your shyness and social anxiety. The most important thing here is to be completely honest with yourself.

Day 2: Prepare

Soon you will be going out to put yourself in a social situation, but instead of throwing yourself out there from the start, take some time to mentally prepare yourself for it.

First, determine an exposure activity you will begin with. This does not have to be something elaborate and extremely intimidating. Consult the hierarchy you created on Day 1 and choose one of the least anxiety-causing items, to begin with. This can be as simple as going to a fast food restaurant to order some food or your weekly meeting at work. But don't panic just yet; there are a few more steps to take before you embark on your exposure activity.

Take some time to prepare yourself for the situation you are going to go into. Have an idea of what you will say in the situation. Determine some strategies for starting a conversation that you can use such as Inspirations, Observations or Positive Talk. Think of some of the safety behaviors that have become a habit to you. Do you often hold yourself stiffly to avoid shaking? Do you avoid eye-contact? Make a note of the safety behaviors you use so you can remember them when you find yourself in a social situation.

Finally, set a goal for yourself for your first exposure activity. This could be as simple as making eye contact with someone and smiling. Or you can be more elaborate and challenge yourself to say hello and start a conversation. The main thing is to set an achievable goal that you know you can stick to.

Day 3: Exposure Activity

Now is the time for your small exposure activity. Say for example today is the day you will go check out a book at the library. It may seem easy, but being surrounded by people and having to interact with the person who will check out the book is intimidating to you.

Before you actually go out, give yourself a little pep talk. Start by acknowledging the anxiety you are experiencing. Tell yourself this is what you are experiencing right now but it is okay to feel these things, you will not let them stop you from achieving today's goal. Banish the negative thoughts you may be having. If you are telling yourself that you can't do this, saying something like "I am not capable of doing this," think about evidence to the contrary. What is actually stopping you from doing this? Is there any real reason why you can't do it? No, there is not. Tell yourself that you can and you are capable.

Entering the exposure, in this case, the library, keep these little things in mind and argue back at the negative thoughts that creep into your mind. As you approach the librarian to check out the book, think about those safety behaviors that you determined on Day 2. Make an effort to stop doing them.

Finally, achieve your goal. Smile, introduce yourself, say hello, and make small talk while they are checking out your book. When you leave, let out that sigh of relief. Achieving your goal, however small or large it is, can seem intimidating before you get started. But by the time it's over, you will feel a sense of accomplishment and a little bit of that anxiety you have going into social situations will subside.

Day 4: Evaluate

Make this time to reflect on the effort that you put in during Day 3. This can even be your journal entry for today. Think about how you did during the exposure. Did you speak clearly? Did you make eye contact? Did you accomplish your goal for the day? Also think about how it made you feel. What were your thoughts and feelings before, during and after the exposure activity? Maybe during it, you felt nervous and you felt like turning around, but after finishing you felt a sense of accomplishment. Then think about what you can do differently. Write down some ways you can improve your performance the next time you are in a social situation.

Day 5: Begin Practicing Healthy Habits

When it comes to overcoming social anxiety, it's not all about focusing on the exposure and the mental aspects of the issue. Working on your physical self can do wonders for overcoming social anxiety as well. Getting enough sleep, sticking to a healthy diet and getting enough exercise will not only make you feel better physically, but mentally and emotionally as well, making it easier for you to get into the positive mindset that comes with exposure to socializing.

Make a commitment to get at least eight hours of sleep every night. Cut back on the junk food and eat healthy meals, cooking at home is even better. Also try to exercise t least two or three times a week.

Day 6: Commit

One of the best ways to continue your exposure is to find a social activity that you can keep going to that will force you to have to interact with others. Research activities you can get involved in that will allow you to socialize regularly. These can be any kind of club or a group such as a group exercise class, a cooking class, an art class or book club meetings.

Once you find an activity that you have the time for and that you can easily get to, sign up for it. Put it on your calendar, make a payment or contact the organizer. This way, you have already made the first step and there wouldn't be any point in going back on it.

Day 7: Prepare For A Bigger Exposure

You have done a small exposure activity and you were successful at it (or maybe not, that's okay too). Now it is time to kick it into high gear and do something a little more intimidating. Consult your hierarchy again and find something on the higher end of the list that you can go to, or you can pick that meeting that you signed up for in Day 6.

Determine potential stressors that can come with the activity. If you are going to an art class, you might be worried about things like people judging your project or someone asking you a question that you don't know the answer to. Also, come up with solutions or mindset changes to these potential stressors. Remind yourself that everyone is there to learn and you may not be the only one who is worried their work will be judged. If someone asks you a question that you are unsure about, just be honest with them.

Make it a goal to hold a conversation with at least one person there. To help with this, prepare a list of questions or conversation topics that are relevant to the activity. In the case of the art class, this can mean asking about their attendance at the class, their art experience and the project they are working on. Try to memorize some of these so that you are prepared to talk to anyone there.

Day 8: Major Exposure

It is time for that big exposure activity and while this can cause you immense anxiety, remember the first exposure activity you did, how well you did on it and the things you listed that you wanted to do differently. Give yourself that pep talk and make a commitment to your goal.

Use the strategies you laid out to start a conversation with at least one person. Going off of the art class example, introduce yourself to the person you are sitting next to. Take yourself through the four conversation steps: exchanging formalities, observing, getting personal and using their responses to keep the conversation going. Also, just relax. As the conversation goes on, you will likely become more comfortable and you may just make a friend that you can look forward to speaking to during these classes.

Day 9: Evaluate Your Progress

Like your minor exposure activity, evaluate the progress you made during this one and compare it to the first activity to you. What made this exposure different than the first one? Did you put into practice any of the goals you wanted to accomplish from the last one? If so, how did that turn out? Think about what you managed to improve on from the first exposure activity and what you can improve on going forward.

Day 10: Rest

Putting yourself into a social situation against all of your fears is very difficult. It took a lot of courage to put yourself out there and you might feel mentally exhausted. This is a day to just focus on yourself. Do activities that you enjoy to just relax and take your mind off your fears. Don't think about the nerves that appeared during your exposure or what you may have done wrong. Only focus on the positives and the sense of accomplishment that comes with conquering your fears. Make the commitment to continue this pattern of decreasing your shyness.

The Number One Way To Learn How To Connect With People

There are so many things you can do to help you on your journey overcoming social anxiety. From various kinds of treatments and therapy to exercises you can do on your own and memorizing steps for having a conversation and questions and topics you can bring up during that conversation.

But the one way to connect with people, the one way to overcome social anxiety and become comfortable with speaking to new people, is to just go out and keep talking to people. The more you go out, the more you put yourself in social situations, the more you socialize with people on an everyday basis, is to just keep trying to talk to new people. There is no other substitute for exposing yourself to situations and learning than by trial and error.

That's not to say it will be easy. Social anxiety has prohibited you from really utilizing your social skills for years up to this point; there is no way it is going to simply disappear overnight. There is certainly a lot of work you can do on your own in the comfort of your own presence, but this doesn't give you experience with interacting with others. Making an effort to put yourself out there as often as you can is the best thing you can do to make yourself comfortable with socializing. [7]

One of the things you can do to help encourage yourself to go out and interact with people more is adjusting your beliefs about socializing. Socially anxious people have a tendency to focus on the negative outcomes of socializing. They usually find that social situations go better if the negative outcomes they predicted did not happen, but everything won't always go the way you expect it to.

Sometimes you will encounter people who are not very nice and are not interested in speaking with you. Understanding that this is possible, and almost inevitable, is a good first step to take. Practice placing them within the broader context of life is crucial to overcoming social fears as well as learning not to overestimate negative outcomes. [7]

Another thing you can do to help you socialize more is to expand the kind of social situations you are a part of. If you are going for social situations by the hierarchy you have established, if you keep going for those on the lower end of the hierarchy, you will not allow yourself to be comfortable with the ones that cause you the most fear.

You can keep doing one exposure activity over and over, but not only will it become monotonous, but your fears of that situation will also subside and you will be comfortable there and not want to try anything else. Expanding the social situations you seek out helps you to be well-rounded. When you adjust your beliefs about the social situations you will encounter, you will find that you will be more encouraged to socialize more and expand the social situations you are a part of.

Conclusion

Shyness and social anxiety can be debilitating. It can have a detrimental effect on your life prohibiting you from making friends, getting a good job and have a variety of psychological and physical effects such as loneliness and depression.

However, the first step to stepping out of your comfort zone and coming out of your shell is recognizing how these conditions have affected your life and more importantly, wanting to do something about it.

So many people suffer from social anxiety. For many people, it begins early in life and they take, on average, 10 years or more to get help for it because of either not recognizing that they have a problem or being afraid of being judged for having the problem. However, it is nothing to be ashamed of and working hard to correct it is important for making changes in your life.

Overcoming social anxiety is not an easy process. The problem did not begin overnight and it will not end overnight. However, with hard work and dedication, it is something that is highly treatable and can be overcome.

Be consistent on your journey to overcome your anxiety. Be active in putting into practice the strategies you find. Be conscious of your mindset daily. Consistency will be key to overcoming social anxiety. Putting together routines, working every day to change your mindset and setting daily goals for yourself will all be essential in the journey before you.

Despite the endless techniques and skills you can try to relieve anxiety, remember the most important thing you can do is to put yourself out there. It can be intimidating, you would probably rather just stay inside and keep to yourself and stay comfortable. But if you want to achieve your goals and have a better lifestyle, the best thing you can do for yourself is to go out and socialize.

References

[1] "Anxiety Facts and Statistics." *Anxiety and Depression Association of America.*

[2] "Anxiety: Stop Negative Thoughts." (2018). *University of Michigan.*

[3] Bressert, Steve. "Facts About Shyness." (2018). *Psych Central.*

[4] Carducci, Bernardo. Zimbardo, Philip G. "The Cost of Shyness." (2018). *Psychology Today.*

[5] Clark, David M. Gelder, Michael. Hackmann, Ann. Ludgate, John. Salkovskis, Paul. Wells, Adrian. "Social Phobia: The Role of In-Situation Safety Behaviors in Maintaining Anxiety and Negative Beliefs." (1995). *University of Oxford.*

[6] Coll, Elizabeth. Miller, Scott. "From Social Withdrawal to Social Confidence: Evidence for Possible Pathways." (2007). *Current Psychology.*

[7] Crozier, W. Ray. Alden, Lynn E. *Coping With Shyness and Social Phobia: A Guide To Understanding and Overcoming Social Anxiety.* (2009).

[8] Ebstein, Richard P. Israel, Salomon. Chew, Soo Hong. Zhong, Songfa. Knafo, Ariel. "Genetic of Human Social Behavior." (2010). *Neuron.*

[9] Dombeck, Mark. "Socialization." *Mental Help.*

[10] "Exploring Your Communication Style." *The Center For Growth.*
Hope, Debra A. Heimberg, Richard G. Turk, Cynthia L. *Managing Social Anxiety: A Cognitive Behavioral Approach.* (2010).

[11] Katnelson, Alla. "Genetic influence over social skills shifts as children grow." (2017). *Spectrum News.*

[12] Kreuger, Norris. Dickson, Peter R. "How Believing In Ourselves Increases Risk Taking: Perceived Self-Efficacy and Opportunity Recognition." (1994). *Decision Sciences.*

[13] Leahy, Robert L. "How To Overcome Your Social Anxiety." (2014). *Psychology Today.*

[14] Markway, Barbara G. Markway, Gregory P. *Painfully Shy: How To Overcome Social Anxiety and Reclaim Your Life.* (2001)

[15] Rayner, Stephen G. Riding, Richard J. *Self-Perception: International Perspectives on Individual Differences, Volume 2.* (2001)

[16] Richards, Thomas A. "Social Anxiety Fact Sheet: What is Social Anxiety Disorder? Symptoms, Treatment, Prevalence, Medications, Insight, Prognosis." *Social Anxiety Association.*

[17] "Self-Esteem." *The University of Texas At Austin Counseling and Mental Health Center.*

[18] Sherman, Ruth. "Understanding Your Communication Style." *Women's Business Center.* (1999).

[19] "Social Anxiety Disorder: More Than Just Shyness." *National Institute of Mental Health.*

[20] "Social Anxiety Disorder (social phobia)." *The Mayo Clinic.*

[21] Speilberger, Charles D. *Anxiety and Behavior.* (1966)

[22] Hope, Debra A. Heimberg, Richard G. Turk, Cynthia L. *Managing Social Anxiety: A Cognitive Behavioral Approach.* (2010).

[23] Tannen, Deborah. *You Just Don't Understand: Women and Men In Conversation.* (1990)

[24] Morin, David. "How To Start A Conversation."
Social Pro Now. (2019)

Conversation Hacks

Direct Answers To Any Difficult Social
Question You've Ever Had

By

Chad Collins

Introduction

Don't you wish that you had some sort of hack to improve your social skills more easily? If you are like most people, you struggle with social interactions. You may feel comfortable and even totally outgoing around close friends and family, but you are not that way in every situation. Your lack of social skills has made life more challenging and you feel like an awkward failure. If only there was some easy way to become more social and likable....

Oh, wait, there is! There are actually countless social hacks that can elevate your conversations from banal and boring to dynamic and enriching. You can make friends more easily, get business partners more readily, and feel more confident about yourself with these hacks. You can navigate tricky social situations that get the best of you and avoid the awkwardness that brings you down. This book has dozens of hacks that can make your social life soar.

Why should you trust me? Well, I have been in your shoes. I was awkward and geeky at one point. When I got into a business role, I realized that my lack of social skills was holding me back. So, I embarked on a mission to improve my social skills. Years of research and practice have led me to build my business from the ground up, make several lasting friends, and even get married. Now I want to share my secret recipe for social success with you.

As you can see from my story, social skills are the key to your success in life. You will not get far if you continue to be awkward and drive people away. Building good relationships starts with having excellent conversations and convincing people that you are a likable person. Anyone can have social skills. You just have to learn them and apply them. The results will astonish you.

I promise that by the end of this book, you will be ten times more social. You will have better conversations, and you will start to make better connections with people. You will even be a better persuader and influencer, getting your way.

Don't put off learning social skills any longer. Start reading now to improve your relationships and build new relationships. You will be amazed at how opportunities open up and your happiness swells.

Part 1: Specific And Practical Conversation Hacks

When it comes to making new friends, finding new business partners, recruiting clients or investors, and dating, conversation is what starts it all. With the exception of your family members, everyone you meet starts out a stranger. A conversation can change them into important people in your life. In fact, if you think about it, every relationship (except with your immediate family members) started with a conversation.

A conversation is far more than an exchange of words. It is an exchange of information and emotion that helps you get to know someone and show that person who you are. That sets up the framework necessary for a relationship to start. Early on in the relationship, a series of conversations enable both parties to determine if the relationship is worth pursuing and what nature it will take.

Obviously, conversations are absolutely critical to forming relationships with others. If you want to get to know anyone besides yourself, you need to have conversations. But simple conversations about the weather are not going to create much of a connection. A deeper connection is possible with some conversational hacks that enable you to actually get to know someone and convince him or her that you are worth getting to know.

What does science have to say about conversations? A Princeton study has concluded that conversations are not just verbal exchanges, but rather a sync-up between two minds [1]. Different parts of the brain, including those parts involved in processing the meaning of language, will activate. Two people who share similar communication partners and ideas will have brain activity sync up, essentially causing them to think the same way. This allows for a smooth flow of communication that does not cease into awkwardness. If you create that sync with someone, naturally a bond forms that can become a relationship of some kind.

What is even more interesting is that distinctive coupling was found between the brains of people telling life stories and people listening [1]. That means that when you tell or listen to a story, you start the process of this "mind meld." The result is that you feel infinitely closer to the other person. Stories are crucial elements of every culture in the world, and of every conversation. Being able to listen and tell stories are critical factors in making relationships with others.

Creating a mind meld is your ultimate goal of any conversation. These simple yet powerful hacks are easy ways to start the process. Take conversations to the next level and make them mean something.

Don't Be A Stranger

Do you know the number one mistake people make in conversation? They don't initiate conversation.

Basically, they don't even try. And you already know the commonsensical wisdom that you if you don't even try, you can't succeed.

Think of the people in your life. You may have some people that you talk to every day. You know them well and you know the ins and outs of their lives. Then you have acquaintances that you speak to occasionally out of politeness. You have the people you speak to when you have to, such as co-workers. Then there are the not-so-distant strangers, the barista who serves you your morning cup and the garbage man who collects your trash. They are in your everyday life but you don't know much about them because you don't speak to them beyond the necessary few words for your transaction. And finally, there are distant strangers, people whom you have never met and probably never will again, such as the guy next to you on the bus or the woman behind you in line at the grocery store. In fact, I am willing to bet that most of the people in your life are people you barely speak to.

But what about all of these people you don't talk to? From the co-workers you keep at arm's length to the distant strangers, these are people with stories, things to say, and connections that could further your goals in life. You have no idea if one of them might have the potential to be your next best friend or your new business associate. You will never know unless you try to talk to them.

So, don't be a stranger! Strike up a conversation with the person next to you on the place or the person in line. Find out what they are doing, who they are, and whatever else they want to tell you. You might be amazed at how these people can open up opportunities for you or tell you great stories that stay with you for years to come.

One time on a train ride, I was focused on my book, ignoring everyone else. The gentleman sitting next to me did not say a word to me the whole ride. I eventually glanced up from my book long enough to see that he was wearing a shirt from a small coffee place I go to often. I decided to set my book aside and strike up a conversation with him. Not only was he my neighbor, but he was also an employee at my favorite coffee joint. He gave me a free ride home from the train stop, saving me money on a cab, and he told me he would toss me a discount on coffee if I ever came in on his shift. Now we see each other now and then and we always have a little conversation. Just by talking to this man, I was able to save money on transportation and coffee and make a friendly acquaintance with one of my neighbors.

The people around you have a lot to offer. But they will not always initiate conversations. You cannot hang back and expect people to come to you because people are not programmed to talk to strangers. If you make the effort to start the conversations, though, almost everyone will respond. Then you may just find an amazing new person to add to your circle. Talking to new people is the only way to make them notice you and start new relationships that you may never have started otherwise. You might really benefit from these people, more than you ever expect. The person who was a stranger on the train one day might just become someone you can't live without a few months later.

In a study on how people initiate conversations on public transit, the researcher, Ole Putz, developed two theories for how people start conversations: The first is that they relax the rule against talking openly with strangers if there is a disruption in travel [2]. For instance, if the subway breaks down or bad weather creates a delay in a flight, fellow passengers are free to grumble to each other about the disruption. This can start a conversation. The second theory is that people notice things about each other that they have in common, such as another person wearing a concert T-shirt for their favorite band [2]. The latter theory proved to be the most common reason that two strangers found connections on public transit [2]. These two things can enable complete strangers to talk.

Therefore, use this data to your advantage. Use a disruption in travel or some circumstantial occurrence as an excuse to start a conversation, such as commenting on the music playing in an elevator or remarking how bad the weather is. That is an acceptable way to start a conversation with a complete stranger.

Otherwise, observe the stranger for clues about him or her. If you recognize the book he is reading, comment on it and talk about the book. If you like her outfit, say so. These comments can break the ice and allow for a conversation.

Finding things in common makes a mind meld even more likely and possible [3]. Similar neural responses to things are indicators of friendship because people like having things in common. If your neurons start excitedly firing over model trains, you are more likely to bond with someone who also gets excited over that as well. Finding similar interests, hobbies, or even relating to each other about places that you have both been to make for excellent conversation. For instance, if someone's luggage says "Paris," you can ask, "Have you been to Paris?" When the person says yes, you can talk about your experience in Paris or how you have always wanted to go there. Right there you have something in common to talk about.

Another great way to bond with someone is recognizing some cultural similarity. Say you recognize their accent as being from your home town, or you know the foreign language they are speaking in. You can pipe up about how you once lived there or you know the language or you studied that language in school. Apply whatever cultural or linguistic commonality you both share. Finding members of your own culture or background often feels like finding a friend in a sea of strangers. It instantly bonds you both.

It may also be time to finally talk to that barista or server you see every day, that guy who rides your elevator every morning, or that neighbor you always pass in the hall. If you have multiple interactions with someone, the natural barriers against speaking to strangers are eroded and a conversation will be more natural, less awkward. You may also have more of a bond already due to the mere exposure effect, a scientific phenomenon where someone becomes more attractive to you the more often you see him or her [4]. Finally, you have more of an ice breaker since you see each other often. It can be a lot easier to finally ask someone you see every day, "So I see you around a lot. What's your name?"

Most people are shy, or at least reticent to talk to strangers. They are just as afraid of rejection as you are. And if you think about it, the odds of being rejected or brushed off by a stranger are higher than someone you know. Most people won't take that risk because they don't know if it's OK to talk to a stranger or how to break the ice. You can set them at ease by breaking the ice yourself. Then you allow them to feel comfortable talking to you and they like you more.

If you are rejected by a stranger, don't take it personally. Some people just don't feel like talking because they are busy, rushed, shy, or having a bad day. Some people are just rude and unfriendly. For every person who rejects you, there are probably two who will welcome a conversation with you. You won't know unless you find out. You can minimize your chances of rejection by reading someone's social cues. These social cues are usually obvious. A person who has his arms crossed and headphones in probably doesn't feel like talking. A person who is looking around or who makes eye contact with you and smiles is more likely to want to talk.

Maybe the stranger is not giving any social cues. In this case, test the waters by making eye contact first and smiling. If the person responds in kind, you can break the ice. If the person dodges your look, turns away, glares at you, or puts headphones in or pulls out a book, you should probably just not bother.

Ask Away

Many conversations can start by simply asking for something. Persuasion also works this way. If you want something, ask. You (almost) never get what you don't ask for. So, ask! You either end up in the same position you were already in or you end up much better off.

How To Get What You Want

If you want to get to know someone, just ask. Then you find out if the person reciprocates the interest. Asking to talk or asking questions to get to know someone will break the ice.

If you want something from someone, such as a favor,

then ask. The worst they can say is no. Your boss is not going to give you any vacation time unless you ask. You often have to state a need before someone can accommodate it. Remember that no one is a mind reader. No one will just hand you what you want, assuming that you want it. You have to make the need known.

For the longest time, I was terrified to ask my boss for a raise. I was so sure that he would fire me on the spot. One day, though, I heard another co-worker got a raise. I asked him how he did it and he said, "I just showed the boss what I've been doing for the company and asked if I could get a reward for my efforts." I realized then that I had to ask, because my boss wasn't going to just come up to me and offer me more money. So, I prepared a presentation proving my value to the company and then I summoned the courage and asked him for some time. After my presentation, I asked for my raise. And guess what? He said yes. He never would have given me a raise otherwise. He didn't even realize that I wanted one because he is not a mind reader.

Asking is the first step. But it doesn't guarantee you what you want. You may have to push further and use some persuasion. Persuasion is a huge subject beyond the scope of this book, but there are a few basics that you should always use.

The first is proving how getting what you want benefits someone. If you're asking a girl out, for instance, show her how she will enjoy time with you and what you can do for her on the date. Or if you are asking for raise, show how you deserve it and how a raise will keep you invested in your work. Focus on the other person's benefit, not your own. No one cares about how you will benefit. They only care about what they get from it. Prove that someone will get something from doing what you want and you will probably get approval.

You must always make someone feel motivated to

want to help you. No one is going to do something for you unless they have a valid buy-in. You can do this one of two ways: get someone to like you or use Maslow's Hierarchy of Needs for motivation.

The principle of getting someone to like you was first proposed by Dr. Robert Cialdini in his famous six principles of influence. If you make someone feel that they like you, then they want to do favors for you [5]. Another Cialdini principle is called reciprocity, wherein you do someone a favor to get one in return [5]. Create a you-scratch-my-back-I-scratch-yours situation. The person likes you for doing him favors and benefiting him so he is inclined to do the same for you.

Maslow's Hierarchy of Needs involves appealing to someone's needs on a scale [6]. People are motivated by how they perceive their needs will be met by you. If someone sees a way to benefit from helping you with minimal cost to him- or herself, then he or she will gladly do it. The hierarchy starts with basic needs for survival – food, water, shelter. Most people in Western countries have these needs met, but you may find that offering to buy someone food or giving someone a place to stay can motivate them to help you out somehow.

The second level involves the need to feel safe [6]. Improving someone's sense of safety may be as simple as defending them from bullying or promising to keep a secret safe. You can offer someone emotional security by reassuring them about how well they are doing or praising them.

The next level is the need to feel as if they belong and are loved [6]. Offering someone friendship is a good way to get them to want to help you because you are satisfying this need. People want to be liked. If you make someone feel that you will like them more in exchange for a favor, then you may just have your in. However, this usually doesn't work on secure people who already have high self-esteem because such people do not require your approval to feel good about themselves. It only works on insecure people who make it clear that they are desperate for friends or people who admire you and seek your friendship.

Esteem is the third need. This is where someone needs to feel valued and good about themselves. Flattery and praise play in here. Telling someone that he is doing a great job can motivate him to want to do an even better job by helping you. In fact, it has been found that when you praise someone, they are more likely to try to please you to get more praise [7]. In a study, students complimented women who wore blue to class, and noticed that the number of women wearing blue went from 25% to 38% [7]. Then they started complimenting those wearing red and the number of women wearing red skyrocketed 11% to 22% [7]. If you praise someone, they will repeat the behavior and try to keep getting praise. You can incur their compliance simply by complimenting them.

Plus, it has been found that people really can't tell between sincere and insincere flattery [8]. A study of people who used flattery in the workplace showed that they were rated as more competent and better at their jobs than those who did not use flattery, regardless of how sincere the flattery was [8]. Any form of praise works. You can mean it or not mean it, but act like you mean it. For instance, if you want to flatter your least favorite co-worker, you may struggle to find things that you sincerely appreciate about her, so point out something that she values highly. You might praise her organization abilities if she is a neat freak, for instance, since her habits indicate she cares highly about being tidy.

The final level is the need to be self-actualized or feeling like one is fulfilling his or her full potential in life [6]. People usually only focus on this need when they have satisfied their other needs. You can satisfy this need by telling someone how their efforts will further their career, help them help the community, or open new opportunities. You can also tell someone how he is in a great position to help you and he can really improve your life, playing to his power and how far he has gotten in life by his own work.

The second part of influence is showing someone that they will suffer little cost from helping you, or that the cost is worth the benefit. Asking something from anyone poses a problem, in that they must expend some sort of effort or resource on you. Make this cost seem worthwhile. Usually, offering a person a large enough benefit is sufficient to cover the cost. But this is not always the case. As long as you make something seem easy and convenient, you can convince someone to do it.

The final part involves learning what you can about a person. Then you can appeal to something unique about him. For instance, if you have kids and your boss has kids, you might use the reason that you want more time to spend with your children to convince him to let you go home earlier. You might find out that someone hates being left out so you invite him to a party in exchange for a favor. The more you know about someone, the more bargaining power you have.

It is beneficial to find out what someone loves and what someone hates. You can use both in your bargaining. Show him how he can avoid what he hates or gets what he loves by helping you.

Drive Conversations Forward With Questions

Questions drive conversations forward. But while most books on this subject encourage you to ask lots of questions, you may find a repetitive list of questions in real life can feel more like an interrogation. Asking questions the right way is how you can get a conversation to move forward and gain interest from both parties.

First, set some clear guidelines for what makes a

question too personal. Really personal questions make people uncomfortable. You don't want to ask about someone's specific health concerns, for instance, or why someone got a divorce. People will share such information if they want. People have individual limitations on what they are comfortable discussing and what topics are taboo. You just have to get to know someone to find out what topics and questions are acceptable. Let the person guide you by listening to the details that he or she provides. Stop asking about something if the person seems to start fidgeting, looking away, or evading questions.

Second, avoid asking questions in rapid-fire succession. You want to take a more natural, calm approach. Ask a question, listen to the answer, and then think of your reply. Share something about yourself to find a common point of interest. For instance, ask someone if she has pets. When she says she has a cat, say that you love cats and then talk about your own cat. Be sure to share as much as you ask. Let the other person get to know you, too.

A great way to keep a conversation going is to ask someone for an explanation. If they say something that you don't understand, ask about it. If your new conversation partner mentions a band you have never heard of, ask what kind of music they play or even ask to hear a song. Find relevant questions to ask about what someone says. When you do this, you make a person feel as if you really care because you are listening and trying to learn more.

Say someone is an expert on something. There is no better way to start a relationship than to ask him or her about a subject within his or her expertise. For instance, at an art gallery opening, ask the art connoisseur about the art presented. You will not seem like a fool if you profess that you don't know something. Your eagerness to learn will make others want to teach you.

You can even ask people for advice to start a

conversation. But be sure to only ask if you intend on following the advice. No one likes to give advice only to have you argue with them. Ask someone for some input on a situation and then make them feel good by saying, "Thanks! That's great advice. You really helped me."

People all have opinions and they love sharing them. Asking someone's opinion will definitely break the ice. "What do you think of that performance?" is something you can ask someone you were sitting next to at a concert. "What did you think about that play?" can be a good ice-breaker at a game. "What do you think about this place?" is another example. Ask someone what they think and you will hear a reply.

If you can't ask an opinion relevant to a situation you are both in, then ask someone their opinion on current events. People love discussing current events. Since we are all in this life together, experiencing the same things differently, asking people about current events can offer you a wealth of perspectives. It can also shed light on someone's character and help you decide if you want to pursue a friendship or partnership with someone. For example, if you are opposed to a political candidate and someone else loves him, you might not want to push the relationship further because you have fundamental differences in how you feel about life.

One thing people love to do is to talk about their cultures. They appreciate others showing interest and trying to become educated. Don't assume you know everything about a culture just because you have been exposed to it on TV. If you meet someone of a cultural background different from your own, try to ask questions about their customs and beliefs. Ask, "What was it like growing up in that culture?" Never assume someone is foreign. Let the person tell you if he or she is from a different country and then ask about that country and what it is like living there. Don't state stereotypes or make jokes. Just try to learn what you can about said culture.

When you ask questions, try to find out what you share with someone. You want to drive the questions toward getting to know a person and what he or she may share with you. As you already know, commonalities bond people, so your ultimate aim is to find as many as you can. You want to ask about their hobbies, culture, and the like. You can also comment on things you notice about them, such as the book someone is reading on the train. Try to find out if you like the same pop culture icons or follow the same TV series.

Often, just by observing someone, you can come up with some questions to ask. "I see you have a lot of purple in your outfit. Is that your favorite color?" "I see that picture of a cat on your desk. Is that your kitty?" "I noticed that you only eat salads at lunch. Are you a vegetarian?" It is very flattering when you notice details about someone, and it shows you care if you ask questions relating to those details.

Paying attention to details helps you find things in common, too. "I love that team, too!" is an example of how you can break the ice if you see someone wearing a hat representing a specific team. "Who is your favorite player?" is a question you can ask to keep the conversation going.

Form Bonds Over Similar Situations

When you are in a situation with someone, you have a rich opportunity to bond over it. Two people trapped in a stuck elevator can become fast friends because they are sharing an experience that puts them in close proximity and exposes them to the same problems.

When you find yourself in a situation with someone else, use that situation to create conversation. You have a convenient ice breaker: a comment about the mutual situation. The other person is more likely to respond because he is sharing something with you and it would be awkward to not respond if you two are stuck together in the same place. Remember that Putz study about how strangers on a train tend to initiate conversations [2]? That's a prime look at how similar situations can form a bonding point.

Don't Be Selfish

We have all spoken to that selfish blowhard who goes on and on and on about himself or herself. You know how annoying it is. Yet you may do this yourself, simply because it is human nature to talk about yourself. You enjoy the sound of your own name the most, you enjoy talking about things you care about, and you enjoy stating your opinions. In your little world, you are the most important thing that exists; to others, maybe you're not so important, because they are preoccupied with themselves.

Most books on social skills suggest focusing on what other people want to talk about. This is great advice, in that other people will enjoy talking to you if they can talk about themselves, given the point above. Yet it makes for some dull conversations when you just don't care about what they have to say. And what about you? Don't you have the right to talk about yourself a bit and enjoy the conversation?

Well, yes, you will actually have better conversations if you talk about yourself a bit. The key here is finding a nice balance. You want to give and take. There are two kinds of communicators: those who share and those who ask questions [9]. Well, actually, there is a third type: the person who shares and ask questions. When rated on effectiveness, the third type tended to get the best scores [9].

The open sharer will think, "I feel like I'm being interrogated! Will this person ever tell me anything about himself?" when speaking to a question asker. The question asker thinks, "Wow, will this person ever ask me anything?" The two styles don't mix.

Therefore, blending them tends to remove that problem. You are not interrogating anyone and you are sharing things without seeming selfish.

So, basically, you want to ask questions to get the other person to share things about himself. You want to show an active and genuine interest, which looks like praise to the other person. And you want to listen well. But then you want to give some details about yourself too. Try to fit them in where they are relevant, such as agreeing with someone or sharing a story similar to the one someone else shared. You want to say, "I went through that too" or "I have a dog too."

Don't be selfish when it comes to conversation. Don't hog the spotlight for too long. A few minutes is the maximum amount of time you should hold the spotlight before giving it back to the other person. That way, you are sharing and letting the person get to know you, but you are not boring the person to death.

You also want to spread the love, so to speak. You want to promote and recognize others as much or even more than yourself. You come across as conceited and obnoxious when you are constantly self-promoting. If you spread the love a bit, you make others feel esteemed, which is one of Maslow's hierarchical motivators [6].

People love praise, plain and simple. In fact, so much so, that a study about the neural responses teenage girls have to maternal praise and criticism was astonishing: girls who hear criticism develop brain activity similar to depression and often go on to develop depression and anxiety issues as adults if they hear constant criticism [10]. People are hardwired to hate criticism and to love praise, so you want to dole out the praise.

How do you do this? It can be as simple as offering someone a compliment on her outfit. Or it can be more significant, such as praising someone's heroic efforts spearheading a donation campaign or someone's amazing contributions to the company. Tell someone how great or strong they are and give some real evidence as to why you think so. Tell the person, "We couldn't be here without you. Your work is so important." The flood of oxytocin and dopamine that someone gets from hearing such words will make them love you so much more.

The thing about doing this is that others will love the attention. Then they are likely to return the favor by the rule of reciprocity [5]. So, while you do something selfless by directing praise and attention toward the other person, you will likely benefit. Plus, you make the person feel good so that he or she will like you more. Then you can reap even more benefits from the relationship.

As long as your praise does not sound insincere, people will appreciate it. Realize that compliments less meaning with use, so repeating the same compliment or telling different people the same compliment makes its power wear out [8]. You want to give out unique compliments and at least try to make them sound genuine.

Flavor Your Conversation With Enthusiasm

When someone asks you how you're doing, answer with "Fantastic!" or "Super!" or "Wonderful!" instead of the usual "fine" or "good." These adjectives just sound better and will really engage the person you're talking to and others around you. Try it out and notice how people always have something to say if you say more than "Good."

I love to tell people that I'm doing fantastic. They perk up when they hear this. They say things like, "Why are you doing fantastic?" I just said something unusual that is also positive. It captures others' attention.

There are other ways to be enthusiastic, too. Say someone invites you out for drinks after work. "OK" with a glum face is not very comforting to the other person; it makes him think that you don't really want to meet up for drinks. But if you grin and say, "You bet!" then you seem more interested and that comforts the other person that you really want to spend time with him.

You want to always respond to others with enthusiasm. Respond to their questions and stories with keen interest. Say yes emphatically. Talk animatedly. Use more interesting words than the dreary ones like "OK" and "I guess" and "good."

Be Inspirational

One conversational hack is to inspire others. When you do this, you make others feel amazing, like the world is theirs for the taking. You goad people to act and feel confident. The result is that you make people like you because you give them that inspirational push to be better in life.

Being inspirational also helps you become a better public speaker. A bored audience is not going to feel the urge to act. A worked-up audience will. You want to inspire people when you talk as practice for when you might need to inspire an audience, give someone a pep talk, or even sell a product to a reluctant customer.

Inspiring an audience or a person is about helping them see *their* vision. Not yours. Your vision has little import for others, but if you speak to their visions, you are speaking in terms they can understand. Imagine if you are trying to inspire a group of people to sign a petition. Talking about how you believe in this cause and you want to see change won't mean much to others. But if you talk about how it will impact their lives and help them move forward, you make it clear why they should care. You can get them inspired to sign the petition if they see how they will benefit or how they will be responsible for bringing about the change they want to see in the world.

Dale Carnegie said it best: Dramatize your ideas [11]. Some showmanship is in order when you are inspiring others. Compare the difference between a dreary PowerPoint and a dynamic one. If you want people to care about what you have to say, then you want to make them *feel* something. Offer them an experience or show them shocking images or speak about the suffering of mankind. Carnegie uses the example of a rat poison company using a display with live rats to successfully boost their sales [11]. This is an example of how you do something to shock people and make an idea real to them so that they feel inspired.

The best way to inspire others is to find out their personal values. Most people tend to commit to something and then stick with it [5]. This principle is one of Cialdini's principles, called commitment and consistency. If you find out how your idea ties in with someone's personal values or causes, then you have an easier in.

It is also easy to inspire people in conversation by finding out their values. A friend who is down in the dumps about his girlfriend leaving may value long-term relationships, so you can inspire him to feel better by pointing out how the relationship benefited him and offered a learning experience to make him better in future relationships. Find out what someone cares about, then target that.

You will find this especially useful in business. If you are approaching an investor, you know that he cares about money above all. So, you want to inspire him to feel that his money is wisely spent on your venture.

When it comes to getting people to do what you want, refer back to some of the influence principles covered before, but also focus on praising these people and making them like you. Doing these things will inspire people to want to please you.

Flattery Will Get You Far

Praise will always motivate people more than criticism. Praise people for doing well and praise those who aren't likely to change. You may just see change in everyone if you offer praise.

Negative comments tend to stick more than positive ones [12]. If you tell someone that he can't succeed, that will stay with him forever. He will forever have a bad taste in his mouth about you because you discouraged him. If you tell someone that she is fat, she will never forget that and will always resent you at some level, no matter how forgiving of a person she tries to be. You make people feel with your words and they tend to remember those feelings for life. Using this knowledge, tread carefully when you speak to people and try to make them feel right.

The best way to make people like you and want to talk to you is to make them feel good with praise. Praise is a huge motivator that encourages people to stick with whatever it is they are doing. It may motivate them to try even harder, too. By praising people, you motivate them to hang out with you.

Use compliments selectively, though. You don't want to just say something like, "You lost a lot of weight!" The recipient may perceive that as an insult instead of a compliment. You don't want to use barbed compliments, which combine an insult with a compliment. Don't point out anything negative or how someone has done better than before. You just want to point out the positives now. Back to the "You've lost weight" compliment, try something more like, "You look great!"

The same old dreary words that everyone says don't have much of an impact. Telling a pretty woman that she looks good won't have as much weight as, "You look absolutely stunning tonight!" Pick words that are more dynamic and unique.

Try to be more specific. "You did great today" is vague. Instead, you want to point out just what you admire about the person's performance today. "I really admire how you reached your sales goal!" or "You really ran well" are examples of specific compliments. They have more meaning because they show a person just what you are complimenting.

Never second-guess what you said or keep adding words to it. Keep the compliment short and sweet. Then it seems more sincere. Going back on what you said, making a big flashy statement, or saying something like, "I think" or "I guess" will make your compliment seem insincere.

Giving the same compliment again and again won't do you any favors, either. Compliments lose steam with time. Instead, find ways to reword the same compliment if you must give it more than once. Otherwise, just give a compliment once and find a different compliment later on.

As a leader, your job is to motivate your followers. People will respond well to praise, no matter how insincere [8]. They are likely to make improvements in their performance in order to earn more praise. You can really motivate workers or team members by telling them that they are doing well, even if they are not. If you don't see the change you want, then you want to let these people go. They are just dragging the organization down and there is no way to motivate them if they don't care about being praised.

You should also praise people after a hard day. Maybe no one reached the goal, but they tried. Acknowledging that everyone tried can be a huge motivator that makes your team members or employees feel validated and more encouraged.

Acknowledge that something was hard and that everyone did their best.

When you have to criticize someone, start with praise to soften the blow. Use more vague terms and suggest ways that the person can improve. Don't just be rude or level accusations at someone. Generally, you don't ever need to criticize someone. Keep negative comments to yourself.

Gratitude Is The Best Form Of Flattery

You already know that flattery is effective at getting people to like you or try to please you, but flattery is not always about compliments. Sometimes showing gratitude for what someone has done is sufficient flattery [13]. Acknowledging what someone has done and showing appreciation is a form of praise that validates a person's efforts and makes them want to do more for you. A simple thank you is often all it takes.

Another trick is to send handwritten thank you notes to anyone who helps you, interviews you, or goes into business with you. It will make you stand out significantly and make the recipient feel much more valued. Something about the written word tends to make a greater impression on the human brain [14].

Always Do Follow-Ups

Marge tells you she has a doctor's appointment. The next time you see her, you ask how the appointment went. Marge is flattered that you remembered and cared enough to ask.

Always follow up on what people tell you. Attempt to remember fine details and bring them up later. People find this highly flattering. Your thoughtfulness shows you care, which makes people want to know you better.

A follow-up can be as simple as remembering that

someone is vegan and keeping that in mind when you suggest places to eat. It can involve remembering that someone has kids or when his birthday is. Always try to remember what you can.

Also, a follow-up can include touching base after you speak to someone. You exchange contact information and later on you ask them how they are doing or ask about something they mentioned in the conversation. Even just a, "It was nice meeting you!" is a thoughtful touch.

A conversation is the opening of a relationship. But the relationship won't happen if the interaction ends with the one conversation. You must push for a relationship by finding a way to stay in contact and then following up. Out of sight, out of mind is definitely real. You have to stay on someone's mind and make them continue to notice you to become part of that person's life.

Furthermore, repeated exposures and follow-ups make you more attractive to someone. The mere exposure effect refers to how someone finds you more attractive the more often he or she sees you. It is estimated that at least five exposures are required to make someone notice you and fifteen to make them find you the most attractive [4]. In one study, five random women who resembled each other attended a lecture at a university. One woman didn't go at all, one went once, one went five times, one went ten times, and so on. At the end of the lecture, students were asked to rate pictures of the women from least attractive to most attractive. The woman who had attended the most got the highest rating. To make someone like you, you must let them see you at least fifteen times.

Open-Ended Questions

Some questions are close-ended, meaning that they lead to only a yes or no answer. They don't invite discussion or detail. The conversation ends with that question, unless you want to ask another. Open-ended questions invite more discussion and keep the conversation going.

Consider the difference between these two questions:

"How was your day yesterday?"

"Good."

"What did you do yesterday?"

"We played volleyball and went to a barbecue place for dinner. We had the best ribs ever."

The first question is easy to dismiss with a monosyllable. But the second invites the person to share details that you can respond to. Always stick to questions that are open-ended because they keep the conversation going. Close-ended ones cause the conversation to die.

"Tell Me More"

This single phrase is one of the greatest conversation hacks in existence. Use it and use it often. When someone tells you something, smile and say, "Tell me more." Or some variation of that phrase. This invites the person to keep talking. It is also flattering, because it proves that you care and you are paying attention. Inviting a person to keep talking about something he or she is interested in causes the person to enjoy the conversation more.

The Emotional Contagion Of Conversation

Emotions are unbelievably contagious, even worse than the common cold [14]. The result of a Princeton study has concluded that the emotion you put out in conversation will affect others. Therefore, you can set the mood for a conversation. If you want people to feel good talking to you and to come back for more, well, you may just want to exude a cheerful and positive mood to make others happy. A gloomy mood will just bring everyone down.

The way you speak indicates your mood. If you are complaining, for instance, you project a gloomy or negative mood. The subjects you choose also affect the mood. Everyone around you will reflect that mood. Most people are not interested in standing there listening to someone complain, nor do they want to feel blue from a conversation about your dog dying.

If you want people to like you, you want to make them feel happy. This calls for more positive, happy talk. Talk about light subjects, share jokes and funny stories, and point out the positives in things. Being a positive person means that you are more pleasant to be around.

A lot of people with poor social skills will complain as a way to bond with others. If you complain, others may agree and commiserate with you. The issue here is that people with good social skills don't want to do that. They are in a more positive state of mind. Also, if you build a relationship entirely on commiseration, then you have created a negative and even toxic relationship that does not include much joy.

The secret is to at least pretend to be happy. That will come across in your language and body language. Then others will feel happy. Since people like feeling happy, it only makes sense that causing others joy will make them like you more.

Repeat What You Hear

Reflective listening is a conversation hack that therapists have mastered. It is a method by which you listen to someone and repeat back what they say. Of course, you want to paraphrase their point into one simple sentence. There are several benefits to this.

The first benefit is that you prove that you are

listening. You have absorbed everything the person said without losing the gist of the conversation. This makes the other person feel validated.

The second is that you can clear up misunderstandings this way. You repeat back what you gathered from the person and if you got it wrong, you just showed the person what you didn't get right. The other person now has a chance to correct you. Misunderstandings can be avoided this way and you can avoid working on assumptions. For instance, if someone seems mad and tells you that he is mad at you because of something you did, you can paraphrase it. Show him that you know why you made him mad so that you can avoid angering him in the future. If you missed the point, he will be able to correct you. Then you are able to avoid causing anger in the future.

The third benefit is that you can gather what someone is really feeling to form an emotional connection. You go beyond the words by paraphrasing what the person said and then saying, "You must feel [insert emotion]." The person can then correct you if you are wrong. You gain a better understanding of what the person feels and how the person reacts to certain life events. For instance, if someone is telling you how he was cheated on, you can say, "I am sure you feel very hurt." He can then say, "No, I just feel angry." You now know his true emotional state and he feels better because you understand him.

Always validate what someone says, too. "I would feel that way too" is a good way to validate someone. This is a tip especially useful when someone is venting to you or you are talking to a victim of a crime. It is a delicate way to handle victims because they already feel bad and you are letting them know that they are not overreacting.

Listen With Your Eyes

Half of a conversation is talking and the other half is

listening. In fact, it can be argued that listening is more important than talking. But listening is not just as simple as hearing what someone says and coming up with relevant responses. You need to pay attention to a variety of factors in the conversation.

Watch someone's body language. Does it match their words? A person who says she is fine while crying is obviously not fine, for example. You can notice discrepancies between words and body language and understand more about what the person is actually feeling.

You can also catch subtle social cues that people give. Few people want to be rude, so they might not say, "I don't want to talk about this." But you can tell they want to leave the topic or the conversation by the way they inch toward an exit, glance at the clock, or yawn. Then you can change the subject or politely excuse yourself so that the person doesn't hate you for trapping him or her in a boring conversation for hours.

You can also tell when someone is passionate about something or likes something. Their pupils will get bigger and their gestures grander. They will raise their voices. They will be more animated and excited, with faster breathing. You can tell they care about this topic so you can keep that in mind for the future.

Put Your Body Into It

Seeing how language is so much more than mere words, it makes sense that you need to put your body into your conversation. What you say with your facial expressions, body language, and tone is important.

People are listening with their eyes, too. Your body language is crucial in keeping the conversation going on a pleasant note. You can betray your real thoughts and emotions in body language, which can deter people from talking to you. You may also be giving mixed messages without intending to, which can kill a conversation rapidly too.

Often, people misinterpret your body language. You might be antsy because you are nervous, but someone else could think that you are not interested in the conversation. Be mindful of your body language and try to appear cool, calm, and confident.

The best body language hacks involve leaning toward someone as they speak. Touch them now and then, such as a light touch on the arm as you make a point or laugh together. Make eye contact but look away every twenty seconds to make it seem natural. Keep your body facing someone and keep your arms and legs uncrossed and open. Hold your head up high to show attention and interest. Smile a lot. Nod to validate what someone is saying.

One little trick to help you relax and have more confident body language is to chew gum. No one will think twice about why you are chewing gum but it will calm your nerves.

Talk To Someone Like He Is Already Your Friend

The difference between a conversation that remains cold and formal and one that turns into friendship is the warmth you exude. You can make people like you and feel closer to you if you always speak to them as if they are already your friends. Do this even with strangers to break down the barriers people set up between themselves.

How do you do this? The main key is to just be warm. Offer lots of compliments. Pat the person on the back or touch his arm. Laugh a lot and tell jokes. Share a bit about yourself. Talk easily and fluidly, and keep a relaxed, confident posture.

A study found that certain questions tend to bond people more quickly [16]. These questions are personal without being nosy or rude. There are fifty such questions, some of them being:

What did you want to be when you grew up?

What is your best memory?

What would you do if you found out you had a month left to live?

If you could live anywhere in the world, where would it be?

If you could have anyone in the world, living or dead, as a dinner guest, who would you choose?

What would be a perfect day for you?

Do you ever rehearse what you are going to say before

making a phone call? Is there a reason why you do this if you do?

What are you most grateful for in your life?

How would you choose to die, if you could choose?

What made you fall in love with your partner/spouse?

If you had the chance to learn your future, would you do it?

These questions are interesting and let you get to know someone. But they also erase the boundaries people have. In this study, conversation partners were asked to rate how close they felt to the other person [16]. The group that asked these questions rated a high level of closeness, while the group that made small talk rated a low level of closeness [16].

You can try this activity with someone. But you can also simply talk to them as if you know them. Don't say things like, "I don't know you but..." Say something more like, "You seem like the kind of person who would do this. Am I right?"

Speak about how you admire the person or how you feel grateful for something they have done. Express both praise and gratitude in one breath. This is what good friends do and you can do it with a stranger, too.

Be sure to talk as if you will see each other again. Say "I will see you later" instead of good-bye. Mention that you want to follow them on social media or get their number. Doing this allows you to follow up and give the impression that you want a real friendship to bud from this interaction.

Part 2: Conversational Situations

Have you ever had a conversation that took an unexpected turn or seemed resistant to the usual advice that social skills books give? You probably felt off-kilter and failed to respond correctly. As a result, the conversation ended on an awkward or even sour note and no relationship was born of it. Conversations are all unique and no two will go the same. Learning how to handle different situations is imperative to having good social skills.

This is the exciting part: real-life examples and applications for the hacks you learned in Part 1. A lot of books like this just throw theoretical ideas at you and expect you to figure out how to apply them in real life. This book is a little bit different in that you will see some real-life uses and situations that you are likely to encounter. These situations can throw you off, but after reading this part, you will know how to skillfully navigate them with a minimum of awkwardness and embarrassment.

How To Answer Questions With Information That Doesn't Lead To A Dead End

I'm sure you have encountered this scenario: Someone asks you a question, you answer, and that is that. What you have inadvertently done is create a dead end which halted further communication. Phrasing your answers the right way can prevent that from happening.

When someone asks you a question, avoid giving a yes or no answer. Yes or no does not give the other person much to respond to. They have to make the effort to think of something else to say, and many people won't make that effort. You also make people wonder if you even want to be talking. Monosyllables are characteristic of those who want to stop talking. Providing some details or a story in response to their question is better than offering a monosyllabic answer.

Also, be sure to follow their questions with a question

of your own. For instance, if someone asks, "How are you?" don't just say, "Fine!" Ask them how they are doing. Or if someone asks what team you like, don't just answer with your team, but also ask them what their team is.

You want to give detail, without rambling. Rambling is a symptom of pure nerves. It is common in people who don't know what to say. To avoid it, stick to the topic of the question. Use it as a springboard for relevant topics.

Center your answers around finding something in common with the other person. As he asks questions, he is trying to find out who you are. Show him and then find out who he is. Find things you can relate on. The topics he brings up and the questions he asks are likely related to the things he likes, so you have a solid clue about how to talk to him now.

Some people ask leading questions, which fish for the

right answer. This might be, "What do you think of this weather?" You know that you are supposed to reply, "Oh, it's nice, isn't it?" It may be useful to follow the lead to please the person. But the answer to a leading question can also lead to a dead end, since you don't know what else to say. So, you may switch things up by replying to the leading question with an unexpected answer. This will throw the other person off and make him ask you for more information about why you said what you did. "It's nice, but I like the rain better," could be an example of this.

Learn when to cut in and end rambling, too. When the person takes a breath, you can cut in with something relevant or a question of your own. That way, you are locked in a mono-conversation, where one person does all the talking, often out of nerves.

Dealing With Awkward Silences In Conversations

Don't you hate it when you are talking to someone and then one of you says something that leads to a dead end? Now you're both stuck on this jammed elevator in awkward silence, or you're both on a date feeling really awkward. The thing is, silence creates a major sense of exclusion and pressure to speak [17]. But often both people feel scared to even speak and say something to make things more awkward. This spirals into saying nothing at all and the conversation is over.

First, relax and give it time. Conversations lull and lag naturally, and it's not always because you said something wrong. The other person needs time to think of a new tangent and to process what you have said. Give your partner a few seconds to a few minutes to collect his thoughts. If he really looks like he is not going to say anything, you can then cut in with a new tangent.

Sometimes, it is best to gracefully accept that the conversation is over. The person is done talking; you have exhausted your reserve of things to say to each other. Again, this may not be something personal. It is most common when talking to polite acquaintances or strangers. What needed to be said has been said. You will only make things more awkward by continuing to speak. Give it a few moments and then try to say something. If the awkwardness continues or the other person doesn't even respond, then you can smile and let it go. The other person will appreciate it and your conversation will have ended on a good note.

You can also use this opportunity to exit the conversation gracefully if you no longer want to have it. Use the silence to excuse yourself or suddenly remember something you have to do. Don't make a big deal about it. Just smile and thank the person for talking with you. Possibly exchange contact information. Then say, "Excuse me" and move on. Especially do this at parties or networking events, where you have lots of people to talk to and no time for awkward silences. Remember, you always make someone remember how you made them feel, so don't leave the conversation rudely and make the other person feel as if he or she did something wrong. With politeness and warmness, you can leave the person feeling good about the conversation and liking you even more.

Use the time offered by an awkward silence to think of a new topic or a way to phrase a story. It can be related or unrelated to what you were talking about previously. You may also ask a question to start a new line of conversation. Some people are afraid to start new topics because they feel that they are being rude. But clearly, the old topic has died out. Coming up with a new one will be a blessing to the other person as well as you. You just took the burden off the other person to find something to talk about. I often like to end awkward silences by saying, "So, did I ever tell you this story?" Then I launch into a story about something totally bizarre but amusing that happened to me. It always works.

Even better, think back to the conversation and think of a valid question. "So, you mentioned that you study aeronautics. Can you describe that a bit more? I know nothing about it." This is an example that shows you were listening and using the silence to process what you have heard. The other person can appreciate that and fill in more information. The conversation is reborn.

A smooth commentary or joke about the silence can also be useful. Say the silence starts after someone makes a random joke. You can wait a beat, then laugh and say, "I guess none of us can top that!" Or if you have said something that has shocked the other person to silence, say, "I guess I caught you off guard with that zinger. Want to talk about something else?" Or if someone just said something that is difficult to digest, fill the silence with a brief, "I see what you're saying. I'm just taking a moment to think it over."

Watch for someone's body language to see if you

really did make a mistake. You can tell if someone is offended by the way they pull back from you and look displeased, probably just for an instant. You can tell if you made someone uncomfortable judging by an awkward smile and fidgeting or shifting away from you. If you recognize these signs, then apologize. "I said something wrong and I'm sorry. Do you want to talk about something else?"

Sometimes, an awkward silence will ensue when your mind goes blank and you feel unable to think of something to say. Does this sound like a first date you've had? Chances are, nerves have made you unable to be the smooth social charmer you secretly are. The best solution here is to take three consecutive deep breaths through the mouth, exhaling through the nose. Then laugh and make light of your mind going blank.

For example, once I heard a friend of mine discussing how he was unhappy with a grade he had received on one of his college courses. I told him, "Just speak to your...." Then I stopped. The word I was looking for eluded me. An uncomfortable pause stretched on forever and the guy was looking at me, his eyebrows raised. Finally, just as he turned to his partner and started to open his mouth to say something to her, I thought of the word and blurted it out, "Your dean!" Then I laughed and said, "I was having a brain fart." He smiled and the conversation resumed smoothly. A sense of humor about yourself comes in handy in these situations.

Always rehearse a few things to talk about before you meet with someone if your mind tends to go blank during conversation. You will have a reserve of things to talk about if your mind fails to come up with anything on the spot. That can help you navigate uncomfortable pauses as well.

You can have a few go-to questions to start conversations where they have lulled. Consider these:

- Have you always lived in this town?
- If you could live anywhere, where would it be?
- What made you go into [career or field of study]?
- So how did you meet [spouse/partner]?
- What did you think about [major recent event on the news]?
- Did you hear about [some relevant piece of news or local happening]?
- So, tell me more about yourself.
- When did you start working/living here?
- How do you know [mutual friend/host of party/some other person you both know]?

A final tip is to use the silence to your advantage. Therapists call this the "golden rule of silence." If you don't speak, it pressures the other person to fill the silence. In one-on-one conversation, at least. You won't find this trick useful in exchanges with strangers or at parties where people easily lose focus and start talking to someone else. But when you are one-on-one with someone and you find that they are evading a question or refusing to talk, stay silent. The pressure will eventually force them to blurt something out. This is a good way to find out the truth from someone or make someone come up with a new topic to talk about. It is also a good way to get people to start talking about themselves.

How To Have Deeper Conversations

The problem of having deeper conversations is an age-old one. Everyone can engage in small talk. The problem with small talk is that it is not particularly lively and won't stay with you forever. Think back on your most (positive) memorable conversations. They were probably about your philosophy on life, your passions, or something emotional. You probably don't remember too many of those passing "How 'bout them Cowboys?" or "The weather is nice today, isn't it?" conversations.

It is OK to start conversations with some small talk.

After all, small talk serves as an ice breaker that gets you both talking. Use it as your opener and then segue into something more interesting. Be bold and propose any topics you think might be entertaining to both of you.

Listen to what people say. Allow yourself to be vulnerable to their words. If you express emotional reactions to what people say, then you seem more human and take the conversation to a deeper emotional level. For instance, if a woman is talking about how she lost her son, allow yourself to feel sad and show that on your face. "I am so sorry for your loss. You are strong to have gone through that but no one should have to." This is far better than being wooden. You then may mention a major loss you have suffered to show that you understand and you both share something in common.

As people share things, share some things of your own. A woman might talk about her cat, so you talk about how soothing cats are and how they show better health and happiness results in nursing home patients who get to keep cats as pets. A man may mention golf, so you mention how relaxing golf is and talk about some of the courses in town. The conversation just went from small talk to a related deeper subject matter.

Pick a topic you'd like to get deep about in your mind. Then ask a specific question to get the other person to think about said topic. You might say, "So you mentioned you work in a hospital. What is your opinion on the current healthcare crisis?" Or you might say, "So what do you think happened to create us? Do you believe in the Big Bang, or do you think something else happened?"

Ask people about their lives. If someone is talking about his career, you can keep it small talk by asking, "So do you like your job?" Or you can take it deeper by asking, "How does your job make you feel? What are the high and low points?" If someone mentions that she is not sure what she's doing with her life now as she's between jobs, ask, "Where do you see your life headed?" Think about what someone has said and then ask a question that invites introspection and deeper discourse on the matter.

I often love to start a conversation by saying, "I was walking here today and I was really looking at [some building or monument]. It made me think about how it was built and all the lives it has impacted, all the people who have lived or worked there, all the people who have visited it, all the people who have seen it. That gets pretty mind-boggling. How many people do you think have interacted with that place somehow?" Bringing up history and sociology of places is a great way to start a deep, fascinating discussion.

I will do the same thing when looking at the stars with someone. "It's amazing that most of these stars are dead and new ones have been born that we can't see yet because the light hasn't reached us. These stars are millions of years old. What do you think the night sky looks like now?" Looking to the sky and talking about how fascinating it is can really open up conversations on a deeper level.

If you don't want to get philosophical with someone, at least get into politics or religion. Otherwise, you can get into deeper aspects of their personal lives. People are more willing to disclose personal details the more they talk. As they share, listen well and ask questions about how they feel, or empathize.

How To Gracefully End Conversations

A conversation has lost its luster and now you want to talk to someone else. Maybe it's time to get going. How do you politely extract yourself from a conversation without hurting the other person? Some people tend to view it as a rejection when you end the conversation. But most people will understand and not view it as a rejection if you handle the exit carefully.

The best way to end a conversation gracefully is to find a reasonable excuse to leave it. Ask for directions to the restroom, even if you know where it is. Say that you have to call home. Mention that you have to get up early and must go home. Find some reason that you need to go. People may not take a hint, but if you walk away as you say your excuse, they will know the conversation is over. Be sure to say good-bye and thank you for talking or talk again soon as you leave.

Sometimes, you have no desire to end a conversation, but you have other people to talk to. This is especially true at a party or networking mixer. Ask the person to introduce you to other people in the party. Say, "Who else should I meet here?" Or even be honest and say, "It was great talking to you! Here's my number so we can talk again. Now I need to go mingle." Be sure to smile at the person again every time you see him or her at the party.

You can also reverse this by introducing the person to someone you know. They will start talking and you can smile and walk away. You just passed your conversation off on someone else. You will not look as rude walking away. Plus, you may have just brought two people together who will really like each other. You never know.

Another trick at a party or event is to say, "I'm going to refresh my drink. Do you want something?" The other person nearly always says no, so you are free to go to the bar for a drink and then move on. But if the person says yes, get him or her a drink and say, "It was great talking to you. Have a great night." Then hand them the drink and walk away with a big smile.

If your co-worker or fellow student has you trapped in an endless conversation, you can use work or schoolwork as an excuse. "Well, I have to go get this done. Thanks for chatting and I'll see you later!" You just politely closed the conversation and gave a good reason. The other person should not feel rebuffed at all.

When you meet someone, the conversation will eventually have to close. All good things must end. But that doesn't have to be the end of all interaction. Plan a get-together based on some hobby you both share or invite the person to a party or barbecue you may be hosting soon. Even just say, "Let's get together soon" and then hand the person your card or number. Invite someone to connect on social media. Say, "It was so nice talking to you. If you'd like to talk again, this is my number or you can find me on Facebook." You may even pull out your own phone and have them put in their number or help them find you on social media. You can ask them for their card, too. All of these things ensure a future connection that means the conversation did not go to waste. Plus, you make the person feel better about you exiting the conversation because you clearly want to talk again.

Of course, you don't always have to follow up on these

connections. You can ask for their card or number but never contact them again if you don't want to. Asking for contact information is simply a polite way to end the conversation on a positive note.

When you have exited a conversation at a party or work or some other situation with lots of people, be sure to say good-bye to everyone you talked to before you leave. This leaves a warm feeling with the people you met. You don't seem like you're running away, but rather just leaving because it's time to go.

Now sometimes people will be rude. How do you leave a conversation with someone who is insulting you? That is when you need to be assertive. "I don't appreciate what you are saying and I'm going to walk away now." That's all you have to say. Then walk away. Don't engage anymore. There is no justification for an argument; you probably won't win and you will look bad to others if you stand there arguing with someone. So just leave the conversation.

Other people are rude in that they refuse to listen to your cues and let you walk away. They essentially trap you in conversation. Out of a desire to be polite, you keep hinting that you want to leave, but you can't. Even when you start to walk away, they follow, still talking. In these instances, you should also be assertive. "I really need to go now. Nice talking to you!" Then walk away as fast as possible.

Some people don't intend to be rude but they have no social skills and thus can't pick up on social hints. An example may be someone suffering from autism, or someone who grew up isolated. Don't judge this person or be rude to him or her. Just say, "OK, well I really enjoyed talking to you. I have to go, but thanks for chatting. I hope the rest of your day goes well." Redirection also works well with these types. "I've loved talking to you, but maybe we should go do this instead now?" A gentle prompt to do something else can help you extricate yourself from the conversation.

When A Friend Uses You As A Security Blanket Or Vice Versa

In new situations, people get nervous. They tend to want to hang onto a security blanket. This could be you, hanging onto a friend at a party or new social club. It could be your friend, hanging onto you. The problem with using someone as a security blanket is that you smother the person you are using and you prevent both parties from meeting new people. This can lead to a lot of awkwardness, resentment, and missed opportunities.

Social proof means that if you have a friend with you, you are more likely to make other people want to like you [5]. Basically, by having someone like you, you signal to others that you are likable. More people will follow suit. Consider what happens if you go to a bar alone versus when you go with friends. More people will talk to you if you are in a group, but if you are alone, you might get a few glances but few interactions. This is the principle of social proof at play.

But people tend to overuse and rely on social proof too heavily. In new social situations, they cling to their friends, hoping that their friends will help them navigate the social scene. By doing this, they close themselves off to new opportunities to meet others. They zero in on one person and exclude the rest. If you are using someone as a security blanket, or someone is using you, then you need to end the co-dependency and cut you both free to meet new people.

You should be sure to talk to other people. As you stand with your friend, smile at and greet others. Ask your friend to introduce you to people she or he may know and then start conversations with them. Hang out with these new people for a while until the conversation dies. You can then circulate and meet new people. Touch base with your friend occasionally, since you are here together. Probably every two conversations, you can return to your friend without appearing needy or clingy.

In the event that a friend is clinging to you, start introducing him or her to other people. Then walk away as they start talking. Encourage your friend to mingle if he or she keeps following you around. Understand that your friend is probably feeling very out of place and uncomfortable, so ease him or her by making introductions and including him or her in group discussions.

It is perfectly possible to stick with your friend through an entire social event. Just engage in lots of group conversations and invite other people to talk with you. If your friend is engrossed in conversation with someone, don't constantly interrupt. Find someone else to talk to. Often, group conversations tend to splinter into several smaller conversations, so find someone in the group to chat with yourself. If your friend constantly interrupts you while you talk to someone, invite his or her thoughts and try to make them a part of the conversation you are having with someone else.

You may also make a pact before entering a party to mingle. "We need to meet new people tonight, so let's split up and mingle." This sets boundaries from the start to prohibit clinginess.

How To Talk To Someone Who Is Surrounded By Friends

You may experience the flip side of the issue discussed in the previous chapter: You want to talk to someone, but he or she has a security blanket, or is surrounded by a throng of people. Breaking into that throng just to single out the one person you want to talk to can be nerve-wracking and even unwelcome by the other person.

The first method is to wait for the person to break away from the group. You can then catch this person and ask him or her a question to break the ice. You may also offer to get the person something to drink.

This could take forever, however. And you don't want to stop someone who leaves a group conversation to use the bathroom or talk to someone else specific. You want to instead try to enter the group and talk to them as a whole. Walk up to the group and warmly introduce yourself. Mention, "I heard you talking about [blank]." That way, you can enter the group conversation. Start to focus more on the person you are interested in and ask him or her a direct question. Eventually, if you pay enough attention to him or her, you may allow a one-on-one conversation to form and you can splinter off from the group conversation.

This second method is great at parties, where lots of people are mingling and talking in groups. But it may not work in a group of friends spending time together at a bar. The friends may want to be left alone. A good ice breaker may be to walk up to the person you want to speak to and say, "Hey, I noticed you and wanted to say hi." The person may shoot you down, or he or she may want to talk. It is really hit or miss.

You can also use someone's friends to get to them. As you see one of his or her friends alone, mention, "Who is that [person]? Can you tell him/her hi for me?" Another trick is to send a drink to the person in the group, and then smile and wave when the bartender tells the person who bought the drink. This may cause the person to want to talk to you, but again, this is highly hit or miss.

If you are in a group of friends and you see someone in another group of friends, invite the two groups to join. Go over and challenge them to a game of pool at a bar or invite them to share your table. This can make the situation less awkward since more people are involved. You are not doing this alone.

How To Let Someone Know How You Feel About Them

Say you are having the conversation of your life with someone. You want the relationship to go a certain direction, perhaps a romantic one, or perhaps a friendly one. How do you make it clear how you really feel and what you want without seeming forward or weird?

The key to being an adult is clearly communicating what you want with other people. You save a lot of time by making your intentions clear from the start. However, telling a person you just met, "I think I want to date you. How does that sound?" can grind the conversation to a very terrible stop. There are unique connections where this kind of phrase will work beautifully, but generally, this kind of directness will only make others uncomfortable.

You can state your intentions without being too direct. Say you meet someone at a singles mixer and you have romantic intent. You can say, "I am looking for someone to date." If a person meets you at a random place and asks what you are looking for, be honest without saying specifically, "I want to date you." Then ask the other person what they want. If they want the same thing as you, say, "Would you be interested in seeing me again?" Even if the person says no, you can gain brownie points by giving him or her your card or number and saying, "Well, in case you change your mind, you can call me."

At the end of a great conversation, you can say, "I really enjoyed hanging out with you. I'd love to see you again. What do you think?"

Sometimes, two people are magnetic. This can be true for couples or friends. You meet and without a doubt you like each other. It is clear in both of your words, facial expressions, and body language. In this case, go with social cues. "I think we should be friends. Let me get your number." "I think we should go out sometime."

A first date is an ideal time to state your intentions. Be clear if you are looking for something serious or casual. People will know what you mean, and if they don't, clarify. You don't want to lead someone on or create confusion by being unclear about your intentions. A lot of drama can be avoided and someone will respect you more if you just say what you want off the bat. It's perfectly acceptable to be assertive and say, "I'm not looking for anything serious right now." Don't just say what you think someone wants to hear because you may be wrong. You may be surprised that another person wants the same thing as you. If the other person wants something else, then now they know what you want and how to proceed.

If you are simply not sure where you want the relationship to go, then you don't have to say anything. Just invite the person to talk to you more. Take your time getting to the person until you decide. If the person ever asks, "What do you want from me?" or some such question, be honest that you are not sure right now. Ask for more time to get to know the person and invite him or her to share more about him- or herself.

A lot of people feel the need to make excuses for what they want. "I'm not looking for something serious because I got hurt recently." "I want a serious relationship because I'm already 35 and still not married." "I don't seem to do well in relationships so I just like to sleep around." There is no need to make excuses unless the other person asks. Just state your intentions and leave it at that. You don't need to explain yourself. Most people don't even want to know the details.

You may find yourself in a situation where you decide not to pursue a relationship of any kind with someone. Be as direct as possible and you will avoid hurt feelings. Say something simple and concise, like, "I don't see this going anywhere" or "I think we're better suited for other people." Lying can only lead to more heartache in the future.

Perhaps you meet a girl and you don't want to date her. You tell her that you are not interested in something serious to gently reject her. But then you meet another girl and you fall in love. The first girl later finds out and is devastated that you lied. She would be less hurt if you had simply told her, "I just don't feel a connection with you. I am going to see other people." It will hurt at first, but she will not feel lied to.

When Someone Is Trying To Argue With You Or Has To Be Right

Some people just have to be right at all times. They will argue themselves blue in the face. Dale Carnegie says that the best argument is the one you never have [11]. In other words, don't engage with these people because it is not worth it and you won't win.

If you stand there and argue with someone, then you anger that person. You also look bad to those around you. You should pick your battles and walk away from ones that are not going to bring any value to your life. Most arguments are not worth having. You don't need to be right any more than the other person does. Only harm will come from engaging.

When a person tries to be right, let them. You won't convince them otherwise. Just nod and agree to disagree.

If a person becomes confrontational, let that person look like a fool in front of everyone else. Smile and say, "I don't want to argue right now." Change the subject or use that chance to walk away. You will have saved yourself some face.

When Someone Asks Or Says Inappropriate Things

Have you ever had someone ask you something really personal or just generally inappropriate? Some people advise that you redirect uncomfortable questions back to the asker. But this is actually bound to backfire. Any person who is comfortable asking uncomfortable questions is also comfortable answering them. If you direct the question back to the person, he or she will likely give you details that you didn't want to know.

Instead, practice your assertiveness skills by assertively ending the line of inappropriate questioning. When your nosy co-worker asks about your divorce, for instance, just smile and say, "I really don't want to talk about that." Then change the subject or walk away. You are creating boundaries this way, showing others what is and what is not OK to talk about with you.

If someone says something really inappropriate to

you, just say something like, "That is not appropriate. I don't want to talk about this." You should use this with people who repeatedly bring up inappropriate things or people who are flirting with you. Really, you should use this whenever you feel someone is making you uncomfortable. State that you want to talk about something else or move along. There is no need to keep up a conversation with someone who has no sense of boundaries.

However, some people just don't know any better. A small child does not know that it is rude to ask someone if she is pregnant, for instance. Have some tolerance for these people and gently smile as you tell them, "That is not appropriate to say or to ask people." You just taught someone a valuable life lesson.

When Someone Embarrasses You

We have all been through these moments. A drunk friend humiliates you in front of a person you have a crush on. A family member busts out the photo album full of naked baby pictures of you when you bring your boyfriend or girlfriend over for the first time. A particularly mean co-worker reminds everyone how you failed at a big launch, incurring mean-spirited laughter all around. Someone makes a hurtful joke about you that fails to be funny.

Often, people put you down in public to make themselves feel better. It is a symptom of their own low self-esteem. This can lead to serious social anxiety and mimics symptoms of PTSD in people who have been humiliated [18]. It is a form of emotional abuse that can make you hate social situations. However, just remember that not everyone does this and most people won't even remember what your mean-spirited bully said about you. Even if they do, they probably agree that this person was out of line, but they don't say so to avoid being bullied themselves. Also remember that this behavior is your friend's self-esteem problem, not your own issue.

Someone may also embarrass you without meaning to. A well-intentioned comment that ends up being insulting, a slip of a secret, or some drunken behavior aimed at you is typically not meant to be humiliating. Accept that this humiliation was accidental and

The first thing to do is to look at the person who embarrassed you and say, "Why did you just say that?" This puts them on the spot and tells them that this behavior is not acceptable. It also makes others respect you because you stood up for yourself.

Then you can do one of two things: Walk away and talk to other people or change the subject. Which option you choose is up to you and the level of humiliation you feel. Either way, you save face.

When You Say The Wrong Thing

Since no one on Earth is perfect, we have certainly all

said the wrong thing at some time or another. We either deeply angered or hurt a friend or made a complete stranger uncomfortable. Then we agonize in humiliation for years after, replaying the conversation in our minds and thinking about how we should have done things differently. This is actually normal [18].

Truthfully, you cannot change the past. Kicking yourself over something you said is useless. Instead, take ownership of what you said and try to fix it right after you say it. Give yourself a chance to make things right in the moment.

First, always acknowledge that you said the wrong thing. Even if no one comments on it, they have noticed. You will look bad if you just let it slide. You are not off the hook just because no one speaks up. Instead, say, "I'm so sorry. Can I take that back?"

You may need to give a person space and time if you

really said something horrible. Apologize and then ask the person to forgive you. Leave him or her alone for a while. Wait for him or her to reach out to you. You may consider touching base in a week or two to say sorry again.

Never pin the blame for what you said on others. You might be tempted to tell someone that he is too sensitive for getting offended at a joke you told about him, for instance. That's a form of emotional abuse. Instead, take full responsibility for what you said. "That was wrong of me and I shouldn't have said that."

Don't offer excuses or justifications of your behavior. Nothing you can say will make it right except an apology. By making excuses, you appear to be saying, "I didn't really do anything wrong."

If you say something embarrassing, just make light of it. Laugh at yourself and say, "That was a dumb thing to say. Let me try again." This helps other people laugh along with you and give you another chance to save face.

When You Can't Think Of A Response

Someone just dropped a real bombshell mid-conversation. Now your mind is reeling and you don't know what to say. This can be awkward.

Maybe someone is teasing you and you can't think of a comeback. In this case, just laugh or say, "Wow, that was a good one. I can't even think of a response." Make light of your blank mind to ease the awkwardness of the situation.

Or maybe someone said something powerful. Just say, "Wow. I need a moment to process that" or "That really moved me. Give me a second to think about it." Take a few deep breaths to clear your mind. Then you will likely think of something.

If someone said something grossly inappropriate or offensive, you can give them a look and walk away. This shows them that they can't speak that way to you. But it can also end any chance of future conversations. To be politer, you can just say, "That was not appropriate, now was it?" This admonishes the person without being too harsh.

When people share painful things with you, most people say, "I'm sorry." This is not a helpful response. It is far better to say, "Is there anything I can do?" Most people just want you to listen. You can listen and nod sympathetically. Say something like, "You must feel [blank]" to encourage someone to talk about his or her feelings. You should also compliment someone on their strength getting through a tragedy or other problem.

Don't apologize and don't offer advice or opinions that no one asked for. These comments are always unwelcome. It is also unwelcomed if you immediately jump to talking about yourself. While you may think you know what this person is going through because you have been through something similar, you don't really know what someone is feeling because everyone responds to situations differently. You can say, "I have been through that too and it's rough" just to create a sense of similarity and make the person feel less alone. But don't wax poetic on what happened to you, taking the spotlight away. That is selfish. Instead, focus the conversation back on the other person and let the person get his troubles off of his chest in his own way.

It is not your job in life to play therapist to everyone. If you don't feel like hearing about someone's troubles, you can offer a sympathetic response and hug, then move along by changing the subject.

Sometimes, you don't need to think of a response. Just reflect what you feel with your facial expression.

Show that you are listening with a nod or a touch on the arm. Give a person a hug. You don't always need to be full of answers and witticisms. No one will think less of you for having nothing valuable to say at certain times in the conversation.

You can also fill this mind blank with reflective listening. Just repeat what someone said to give yourself time to process it. You can paraphrase to save time and effort. This makes it sound like you have a response and encourage the other person to keep talking. Meanwhile, you don't have to think of anything to say.

Refrain from making a bad joke or rambling to fill the awkward pause that may come with your inability to respond. That just makes you draw negative attention to yourself. You will look far more respectable if you stay quiet than if you say something dumb.

Hanging Out With New People Who All Know Each Other

A super common and nerve-wracking situation is when you find yourself in a group of people who all know each other. These people are too busy exchanging inside jokes and catching up to pay you much mind. You can feel very out of place.

The first step is to relax. Nerves will prevent you from ever breaking down the barriers you have with these people. They don't know you and they are preoccupied with their other friends. They will overlook you and they are not judging you as much as you think.

Next, try to become part of the group. Don't just be a silent wallflower, standing by the wall and listening without talking. Listen to what people say and respond. Inject yourself in the conversation. Try to find things in common with these people.

Ask them questions, like, "How long have you guys all known each other?" People will love sharing the histories of their friendships. If they all engage in a certain hobby, ask them questions about why they got into this hobby and if that's how they all know each other.

As this group of friends shares things you can't talk about, such as memories, other people in the group you don't know, or inside jokes, you don't need to pretend to keep up. You are an outsider and you are not expected to know what they are talking about. Just smile and wait for the topic to turn. Or propose a topic yourself.

Don't ask traditional questions to get to know everyone. The group will not be receptive to this. Instead, talk like you already know them and participate in the conversations the group has. Talk about whatever the group wants to talk about. Add some stories or jokes that fit in line with what the group is talking about so they can get to know you.

Be friendly to everyone, not just a few people. Even if you get bad impressions of certain members of the group, remember that you are only getting a small snapshot of who they really are. If you are friendly, you make a good impression. Not everyone may like you, but you won't walk away with any enemies.

It may take a few times for a group to warm up to you. The more times they see you and talk to you, the more welcome they will make you feel in the future. Keep coming around. You will eventually be accepted. If, however, you don't seem to share anything in common with the group and you don't have to see them again, feel free to never return to that particular group setting.

When Everyone Is Talking About A Topic You Can't Contribute To

You don't know everything in the world. You may often run into conversations about things you don't know anything about. Don't pretend to know. Express interest instead and listen well.

You may also ask, "Can you guys explain this to me?" Someone may be happy to explain the topic to you. You can also do quick research on your phone in order to participate.

Another tactic is to wait until the conversation appears to be winding down and then propose a new topic you do know about. Don't interrupt a conversation in full swing with some random subject change, as that will be unwelcome. But when people seem to be running out of things to say, you are welcome to introduce a new subject.

How To Respond To "You're So Quiet"

When someone says this, your first instinct may be to explain your behavior. But this is not necessary. You don't have to explain or excuse who you are.

You exude confidence when you own your personality. Just smile and say, "Yes, I'm a quiet person." Brush off this comment because it doesn't really mean anything. It is not usually intended as an insult. Most people use it as a sort of ice breaker, because they can't think of anything to say to the quiet person. Use that ice breaker as a chance to start talking and get a conversation going.

When People Aren't Interested In Talking About Your Hobbies

Not everyone is going to care about your Star Trek club or your favorite sport. When you can't talk about hobbies, what can you talk about? The truth is that hobbies are certainly not the center of the universe and you don't have to talk about them. Most books on conversations drill talking about hobbies into you, and while this is definitely a great topic to propose to find something in common with someone, it fails when your conversation partner has no interest in your interests.

Instead of feeling rebuffed or rejected, accept that not everyone has the same interests in life as you do. Try to find other topics to talk about. Ask the person about his hobbies and compare and contrast them to your own. Or simply switch the subject entirely to current events, work, or the person's life.

When You Are Not Interested In What Someone Has To Say

Nothing is duller than a conversation with someone you don't find interesting. The key here is learning to gracefully change the subject or end the conversation. Since you already know how to end the conversation, let's discuss how to change the subject.

An abrupt subject change signals that you don't share an interest in what the person is saying, which can hurt the other person. Since you are supposed to express interest in others in conversation, you should pretend to be interested. Nod, make a nice comment about what the person says, and listen for a few minutes. When the person pauses, you can find a relevant subject change somewhat related to what he or she was saying.

For instance, if someone is going on and on about rocket science and you don't care, you can take advantage of a lull in the conversation to say, "I always wanted to be an astronaut as a kid. I'd love to explore outer space." It is somewhat related, so it doesn't throw a person off. But it also redirects the conversation.

You may also say, "I don't know anything about that, really. I'm more of a sports guy." That way, you politely tell the person what you are more interested in talking about. He or she may take the bait or may not.

When People Don't Ask About You In Conversations

In this book and in many others on the topic of conversation, you have undoubtedly read the advice to talk about other people. This is a foolproof way to get people to talk, since they love talking about themselves. The kicker is that these books encourage an ebb and flow of talking about yourself and asking about someone else. They assume the other person will ask you questions about yourself or at least somehow try to get to know you. But any person who has had real-life conversations knows that this is not how a large number of conversations go. Many people are self-absorbed or simply don't have the social skills to ask you about yourself, so they monopolize the conversation talking about themselves or droning on about some topic they fancy themselves to be experts in. The result is that you may feel as if your conversational partner is not interested in you as a person, which can sting your ego.

When this happens often, you start to ask yourself if you are doing something to put people off. You may feel like no one cares. Or you may even feel that everyone in this world is selfish.

Stop for a moment and consider the conversations you have had that you can remember. Did every single one of them go this way, or are you selectively remembering? You may be choosing to focus on the negative ones because people tend to focus on the negative experiences they have more than the positive ones [12]. Even rats tend to focus more on the bad than the good in clinical studies and people all tend to do this [12]. The truth is that more people ask about you than you realize, and you just focus on the few selfish ones that do not.

The harsh truth is that if this happens to you in every conversation, you may be at fault. You are not showing people that you are interesting. Thus, they gloss over you, not caring about what you have to say. The easiest way to get over this hump is to interject the other person's monologue with something interesting, find interesting tidbits about yourself to mention regarding what they are saying, or even wear something interesting that invites conversation. Also, raise your voice a bit. Quiet voices tend to get drowned out and overlooked in conversation. Speak first and speak fast.

But it may not be your fault – in fact, it probably isn't. Many people are just more concerned with themselves than others and lack the social skills to even pretend to care about others. You are not boring, but this person finds everyone else besides himself or herself boring. You will find that no matter what you say, this person ignores you or finds a way to twist the conversation back to himself or herself.

There is also often social context to consider. If a group of people is chatting, they tend to not to ask direct questions of you, but rather talk amongst themselves about something in general. A large group of friends does not have the time to catch up with every single other person, preferring to talk together about general topics. You may have better luck getting people to ask about you in one-on-one situations.

People doing activities together tend to discuss the activity at hand, not ask each other questions. They want to get the task done. This is especially true for new activities, where people don't know you. Consider a new group playing tennis. Everyone is focused on the game, not you. No one is going to try to get to know you until the game is over. The end of the game is a good time to strike up some one-on-one conversations as you wash up, pack up, and walk out to your cars.

During certain meetings or get-togethers, people talk about the usual topics, instead of each other. For instance, at an office party, people may be more interested in talking about work and their bosses than asking you about yourself. Conversations often focus on the thing that people have the most in common. A work meeting would be comprised of people who have work in common. Don't take it personally. People who work together may catch up with a good work buddy or two, but they are not going to ask you all about how your life is going.

At parties, people are under the influence and more self-involved, far more interested in what they have to say rather than how you are. Bars and clubs are the same way. Often, these situations don't invite highly personal conversations anyway, since they are loud and crowded and distracting. Don't focus too much on how someone acts when they are in a different state of mind or in party mode.

You may find yourself in situations where you are out of place and so no one feels a connection to you and doesn't experience the need to ask you about yourself. Often, your confidence is poor in these situations because you know you're the odd man out. Your lack of confidence can be off-putting. Try to smile more and be more laidback. Crack a few jokes and don't expect to be the center of attention.

Finally, on situations where the other person is trying to impress you, such as a date or job interview, they may make the mistake of talking only about themselves as an attempt to "sell" themselves to you. Just listen and wait for a chance to talk about yourself. You may have to inject yourself into the conversation. Obviously, this behavior indicates poor social skills and low self-esteem in the other person, who wants to please you to feel confident; you can use this to consider if you want to see this person again.

Consider the conversational style of the person you are talking to, as well. Many people don't like to waste time on small talk and expect you to bring up things about yourself without being asked. This is incredibly common, actually. You should bring up things about yourself without being asked. Bring up things that are relevant and related to what the other person is saying. Show your confidence by being willing to share things about yourself without any prodding from others.

If you do say about yourself and no one acts interested, don't let that get you down. Especially in large groups, you may just not stand out at a particular moment. Try to find more things to say that seem suited for the social situation at hand and keep trying until you get a response. Staying relevant plays to the interests of the other person, making you seem more intriguing.

In one-on-one conversations, if you continually talk

about yourself and still feel that the other person is ignoring you or disinterested in you, this indicates poor social skills on the part of the other person. Watch how they are with others and see if they are the same way to everyone. Even if they act more interest in other people, their rudeness to you shows that no relationship is possible. You should just excuse yourself from these conversations and move on. A million better conversation partners exist out there.

Conclusion

Hacks make everything in life easier. Therefore, when it comes to something as challenging as learning social skills later in life, having some hacks in your back pocket can be life-saving. You can dig yourself out of any awkward or humiliating situation, approach unapproachable people, and turn enemies into friends. There is really nothing you can't do with some solid social skill hacks.

Social skills are imperative to operating at your full potential in life. You can make anything go your way if you know how to handle people properly. The hacks in this book will help you handle any situation that may arise smoothly and without mishap.

No one likes an awkward conversation. It can sour your mood and the entire interaction. But now you won't have to worry about that because you know the secrets to avoid and end awkwardness.

Superficial conversations are also annoying and they

fail to lead to any depth in the relationship. Now you know how to skip the small talk in favor of more profound discussions that lead to more heartfelt connections. Imagine elevating conversations from talking about the weather to discussing your ideas about how to save the Earth from an asteroid or some similar fascinating topic that really shows your personality and the other person's thoughts.

You have also learned how to ask for what you want. You cannot expect to get things if you don't ask, so always ask. You have learned how to gracefully respond to the word "no" and turn negatives into positives. Imagine the doors you can open in life if you start asking for what you want and getting it!

Praising people sparks their passion for talking to you. So, does asking the right questions. You have learned how to open communication, instead of allowing it to come to a dead end. Open-ended questions, relevant conversational shifts, and other such techniques keep conversations from growing stale and then dying out.

Many people make the mistake of focusing on their problems, their visions, and their desires in conversation. Now you know better. You know that to really appeal to people, you must show them how they benefit and how they can get what they want. Only then can you truly inspire and convince people. Only then will you make sensational speeches and appeals that grip people, getting them to come around to your way of thinking.

Enthusiasm, new words, and new topics are all essential ways to get people to like you more. But you can use sneaky hacks from NLP and cognitive behavioral therapy to crack conversations open and turn them from mundane exchanges to dynamic ones. You will certainly be memorable now that you start using these hacks!

Since these hacks will elevate your social life to new heights, you should start using them today. Practice makes perfect, so starting to use these now will cement them as regular staples of your social interactions. Soon you won't even have to think about them, you will just do them. Your life will improve exponentially as you begin to deal with people in a more satisfying way.

References

1. Hasson, Uri. Clicking: How Our Brains are in Sync. Princeton. https://www.princeton.edu/news/2011/12/05/hasson-brings-real-life-lab-examine-cognitive-processing

2. Putz, Ole. How Strangers Initiate Conversations: Interactions on Public Trains in Germany. Sage Journals. 2017. DOI: https://doi.org/10.1177/0891241617697792.

3. Carolyn Parkinson, Adam M. Kleinbaum, & Thalia Wheatley. Similar neural responses predict friendship. Journal of Nature Communications, Vol 9, Article # 332. 2018.

4. Yoshimoto, S. et al. (2014). Pupil Response and the Subliminal Mere Exposure Effect. PLOS One. 9(2): e90670. doi: 10.1371/journal.pone.0090670

5. Cialdini, R. (2008). Influence: The Psychology of Persuasion, 5th Ed. Allyn and Bacon. ISBN-13: 9 78-0061241895

6. Maslow, A. H. (1943). A theory of human motivation. Psychological Review, 50(4), 370-396. http://dx.doi.org/10.1037/h0054346

7. Tesser, M. Advanced Social Psychology. New York: McGraw Hill.

8. Deluga, R.J. Supervisor Trust Building, Leader-Member Exchange, and Organizational Citizenship Behavior. Journal of Occupational and Organizational Psychology. Vol 67, pp. 315-326.

9. Gravagna, Nicole. Question Askers Versus Open Sharers: How Different Conversation Styles Interact. Huffington Post. https://www.huffpost.com/entry/question-

askers-and-open-sharers-how-different-conversation_b_59c5e5d7e4b08d66155042ad.

10. Apperle, Robin, et al. Neural responses to maternal praise and criticism: Relationship to depression and anxiety symptoms in high-risk adolescent girls. Neuroimage Clin. 2016; 11: 548–554. Published online 2016 Apr 4. doi: 10.1016/j.nicl.2016.03.009.

11. Carnegie, Dale. How to Win Friends and Influence People. Pocket Books. 1998. ISBN-13: 978-0671027032.

12. Baumeister, F., et al. Bad Is Stronger than Good. Review of General Psychology, 2001. Vol 5, No 4, pp. 323-370. DOI: 10.1037//1089-2680.5.4.323

13. Kini, P., et al. The Effects of Gratitude Expression on Neural Activity. Neorimage. 2016 Mar;128:1-

10. doi: 10.1016/j.neuroimage.2015.12.040. Epub 2015 Dec 30.

14. Mueller, P. & Oppenheimer, D.M. The Pen Is Mightier than the Keyboard: Advantages of Longhand Over Laptop Note-Taking. Association for Psychological Science. 2014. Vol 25, No 6, pp. 1159-1168. DOI: 10.1177/0956797614524581

15. Adam D. I. Kramer, Jamie E. Guillory, and Jeffrey T. Hancock. Experimental evidence of massive-scale emotional contagion through social networks. PNAS. 2014. Vol 111, Issue 24, pp. 8788-8790.
https://doi.org/10.1073/pnas.1320040111

16. Aron, Arthur, et al. The Experimental Generation of Interpersonal Closeness: A Procedure and Some   Findings.
https://journals.sagepub.com/doi/pdf/10.1177/01 46167297234003.

17. Koudenburg, N., Postmes, T., & Gordijin, E.H. Disrupting the Flow: How Brief Silences In Group Conversations Affect Social Needs. Journal of Experimental Social Psychology. 2011. https://www.rug.nl/staff/n.koudenburg/koudenb urgetal.2011.pdf.

18. Torres, Walter & Bergner, Raymond. Humiliation: Its Nature and Consequences. Journal of the American Academy of Psychiatry and the Law. 2010. Vol 38, No 2, pp. 195-204.

Disclaimer

The information contained in this book and its components, is meant to serve as a comprehensive collection of strategies that the author of this book has done research about. Summaries, strategies, tips and tricks are only recommendations by the author, and reading this book will not guarantee that one's results will exactly mirror the author's results.

The author of this book has made all reasonable efforts to provide current and accurate information for the readers of this book. The author and its associates will not be held liable for any unintentional errors or omissions that may be found.

The material in the book may include information by third parties. Third party materials comprise of opinions expressed by their owners. As such, the author of this book does not assume responsibility or liability for any third party material or opinions.

The publication of third party material does not

constitute the author's guarantee of any information, products, services, or opinions contained within third party material. Use of third party material does not guarantee that your results will mirror our results. Publication of such third party material is simply a recommendation and expression of the author's own opinion of that material.

Whether because of the progression of the Internet, or the unforeseen changes in company policy and editorial submission guidelines, what is stated as fact at the time of this writing may become outdated or inapplicable later.